For Sylvie, with love

Contents

To the Student

This book is designed to help you with your GCSE English Literature examination. It contains a synopsis and an account of the plot, a
glossary of the more unfamiliar words and phrases, and a commentary
on the characters, themes and style and issues raised by the text. An
account of the writer's life is also included for background.

Page references in parentheses are to the Penguin edition of the
novel, edited by Ronald Blythe.

When you use this book, remember that it is no more than an aid to
your study. It will help you find passages quickly and perhaps it will
give you some ideas for essays. But remember: *This book is not a
substitute for reading the text and it is your knowledge and your response
that matter.* These are the things the examiners are looking for, and
they are also the things that will give you most pleasure. Show
your knowledge and appreciation to the examiner, and show them

in serial form, and on his invitation Hardy submitted the early chapters to him in June 1873. He had told Stephen that the main characters were a woman-farmer, a shepherd and an army sergeant, which means that Boldwood did not figure in Hardy's first plans. He completed the novel in the space of a year, and it was published in the monthly issues of the *Cornhill Magazine* throughout 1874. There was a great emphasis on the rural scenes, which Stephen liked, but he was concerned about the handling of Fanny Robin's part in the plot, which might offend Victorian sensibilities.

Hardy himself was obviously fond of his rustic characters (clearly drawn from life), and he wrote to the publishers requesting that whoever did the illustrations for the novel should make the rustics '*intelligent*, and *not boorish* at all'. In addition to the rustics, the novel has vividly drawn major characters in Gabriel Oak and Bathsheba Everdene, and Troy and Boldwood are not far behind them in terms of intensity. There are a number of graphic and finely expressed visual scenes, like the fire and the storm or the less dramatic sheep-shearing scene and the washing. Physical description of this part of Wessex is always present, whether it is Norcombe Hill, the fir plantation or the main Casterbridge Highway as Fanny Robin struggles towards the Union. Consider nature too as providing atmosphere, as when Joseph Poorgrass goes through Yalbury Great Wood with the coffin of Fanny and her child in the claustrophobic and chilling fog. There is Bathsheba's first encounter and entanglement with Troy in the plantation, complemented later by the mesmeric sword-exercise, which reflects Troy's domination of her. In *Far from the Madding Crowd* the realism of the characterization is balanced by the reality of the foreground and background against which the characters live. There is, too, a capacity for grotesque incident, as, for example, when Troy touches Bathsheba through the tent and snatches the note or when, with macabre effect, the gurgoyle spills its waters on to Fanny's grave and washes away the flowers. There is, as always in Hardy, the use of coincidence or Fate, and melo-drama also has its place in the narrative. Troy's disappearance is melodramatic; his reappearance is even more melodramatic and is tragic for himself, for Boldwood and for Bathsheba. All these things make *Far from the Madding Crowd* a richly satisfying and exciting novel, in which the unexpected is set against the natural cycle of the seasons and rustic occupations. The action occupies the period 1869 to 1873. Interest is never allowed to flag, as we move from incident to incident.

Synopsis

Gabriel Oak is a twenty-eight-year-old farmer, formerly a shepherd and bailiff, who has succeeded in leasing a small sheep-farm on Norcombe Hill. One day he sees a beautiful girl on a yellow waggon in the neighbourhood, and a few nights later he observes her with another woman, who turns out to be her aunt, in a hut nursing two cows. On the following day he finds her hat, but when he first sees her she is riding unconventionally on horseback, so he returns it to her later. One night, worn out by work, Gabriel falls asleep in his hut, having left the slides closed. The girl, hearing the howling of his dog, comes to the hut and saves him from being suffocated. Gabriel is greatly moved by the experience, and grateful too. He still does not know the girl's name.

Gabriel has fallen in love. He discovers the girl is called Bathsheba Everdene, and calls to propose to her. Her aunt tells him that she has many young men, which is a lie, but Bathsheba runs after him. Thinking this a positive sign of encouragement, Oak proposes to her, after she has admitted that she hasn't got a young man, but she rejects him since she doesn't love him; soon afterwards she leaves the neighbourhood. Gabriel loses his sheep when they are driven over a precipice and killed by an inexperienced dog. Gabriel goes to the hiring fair at Casterbridge some two months later, but, because he has owned his own farm, he finds it difficult to be hired as a bailiff; he therefore steps down in status and accepts a job as shepherd. He makes for Weatherbury, knowing that Bathsheba had gone there two months earlier. He gets on a waggon, falls asleep, wakes to hear men talking of a woman, who sounds like Bathsheba, dismounts from the waggon, and then sees a fire in the distance. Aided by some workmen, he succeeds in putting the fire out. He finds that the farmer is the girl he loves, Bathsheba Everdene. The men persuade her to appoint him shepherd and then go off to Warren's Malthouse to celebrate.

On his way there Gabriel meets a thinly clad girl, who is obviously distressed, and gives her some money. Gabriel goes on to the malt-house, and is soon accepted as one of themselves by Bathsheba's workmen, who tell him about her family, as well as gossiping generally and retailing anecdotes. News arrives that the bailiff Pennyways has been caught stealing barley. Bathsheba appears at her bedroom window to ask the men as they go home to make inquiries the next day about Fanny Robin, who has disappeared.

The next day a neighbouring gentleman-farmer, William Bold-wood, calls to see if anything has been heard of Fanny Robin. Bathsheba is not dressed well enough to see him, she thinks, but she inquires about him. Shortly afterwards she sees all her men and field-women, interrogates them, and pays them. The plot then takes a sudden turn as we find Fanny Robin at a barracks at night-time. By throwing snow at a window, she attracts the attention of her lover, Sergeant Troy. He agrees to see her the next day.

Bathsheba in her role of farmer appears in the cornmarket at Casterbridge. She arouses a great deal of interest, but Boldwood is conspicuously oblivious of her presence. On Sunday, 13 February, Bathsheba, after tossing up to decide whether to send a valentine to the boy Teddy Coggan or to Boldwood, sends it to the latter, sealed with the words 'MARRY ME'. The farmer becomes obsessed when he receives it, taking it very seriously. Another letter is delivered, this one for Gabriel Oak, and Boldwood determines to take it to him. It is lambing time, and the men gather in the malthouse, which has to be used since there is no lambing-hut. Boldwood delivers Oak's letter, which is from Fanny Robin thanking him for helping her and telling of her forthcoming marriage. Oak identifies the writing on the valen-tine letter as being Bathsheba's. Troy and Fanny, meanwhile, who have arranged their marriage, present themselves at different churches in error, and Troy, frustrated, leaves Fanny in a temper when she does eventually turn up.

In the market-place Boldwood studies Bathsheba, and she becomes guiltily aware of his scrutiny, wishing that she had not sent the valentine. Boldwood, reserved, austere, lacking any lightness or humour, broods on the situation for some time and calls upon Bathsheba on the occasion of the sheep-washing at the end of May. Almost without preamble, he proposes to her. Bathsheba rejects him on the grounds that she doesn't love him, and that anyway he is too dignified and staid for her. She asks for time, and later seeks out Gabriel, wondering what the men think of her being seen with Boldwood. Gabriel is forthright enough to criticize her for 'playing pranks upon a man like. Mr Boldwood' (p. 186), whereupon she orders him to leave.

Gabriel has only been gone about twenty-four hours when Bathsheba's sheep get into a field of young clover and poison themselves. Faced with the agony of watching them die, Bathsheba sends a message telling Gabriel to return, since he is the only person who can cure them. He comes back and saves nearly the whole flock, after which Bathsheba asks him to stay. On the first day of June the sheep-shearing takes place in the great barn. Bathsheba is watching Gabriel's expertise with the sheep when Boldwood calls. Gabriel accidentally snips a sheep, and Bathsheba leaves with Boldwood. That evening at the shearing-supper Boldwood makes his intentions clear, and later Bathsheba says that she will try to love him. Naturally their behaviour has been noted by Gabriel, who still loves Bathsheba, and has also been the subject of comment by the rustics. That night Bathsheba encounters Troy in the fir plantation, his military spur getting caught in her dress in the darkness. He is gallant, flirtatious and full of repartee. Afterwards Bathsheba questions Liddy about him. There follows a description of Troy and his irresponsible attitude; he is a man who lives for the moment. A week or two after the shearing he appears in the fields and helps with the haymaking. He is fluent, inventive and attractive, and he tells Bathsheba that he loved her as soon as he saw her. He makes her a present of the family watch, but she refuses to accept it. Next he appears and helps her with the hiving of the bees. He wishes to show her the sword-exercise, and at eight o'clock on the midsummer evening he does so. Bathsheba is overcome by his dexterity; there is a strong sexual overtone throughout the scene, and Troy leaves her with a parting kiss. She has fallen in love with him.

One evening Bathsheba meets Gabriel when she is out on a walk. He tells her that he is acting for Boldwood in meeting her, but she resents his presumption. He warns her against Troy, and she rebuffs him. She even tries to dismiss him again, but he refuses to go. She meets Troy, and Gabriel checks up on the latter's church-going,

finding that he has told Bathsheba a lie. Bathsheba impetuously writes
to Boldwood to tell him that she cannot love him, and confides in
Liddy her love for Troy. When Boldwood receives the letter he
comes to see Bathsheba as she is setting out on a journey. Boldwood is
bitter with frustrated passion, blames Troy for Bathsheba's change
of heart, and threatens him. Bathsheba becomes scared on Troy's
account. Without telling anyone, she decides to go to Bath to see
Troy. (We later learn that her reason for going was to end her relationship with Troy.) Gabriel and Jan Coggan follow her, thinking
that the horses have been stolen by someone. Not until they reach a
turnpike-gate do they realize that the 'thief' is Bathsheba. She goes
on to Bath, and Gabriel binds Coggan to secrecy about the night's
events.

After a fortnight or so Cain Ball returns from Bath with his own
observations of that place and, more pertinently, his eyewitness account of the courtship of Bathsheba and Troy. That evening Bathsheba and Liddy return. Boldwood comes to call, and is refused entry
by Liddy. Boldwood sees Troy's arrival in the village and supposes he
has come to see Bathsheba. He confronts him and in the ensuing
passionate scene he bribes Troy into marrying Fanny Robin. When
he has overheard Bathsheba's devotion to Troy, however, he offers
Troy money to marry Bathsheba. Troy plays along with all this, and
then produces his trump card, the report of his marriage to Bathsheba.
Boldwood is humiliated and he threatens Troy; he spends an agonizing
night in solitary walking. The next morning Troy appears at the
bedroom window, master of all he surveys. At the end of August
there is a harvest supper and dance. Troy presides, ignores the threat
of rain (despite Gabriel's warning) and ignores his wife's plea not to
give the men strong drink. They all become so intoxicated that Gabriel
is the only one left to deal with the uncovered ricks; before the storm
bursts, he manages to cover the valuable grain, aided and abetted by
a maritally disillusioned Bathsheba. In a terrible moment of confidence she tells Gabriel that she married Troy to keep him for herself,
knowing that otherwise he would have gone off with another. The
next morning Gabriel meets Boldwood and learns to his surprise that
that besotted man has not covered his ricks.

Some two months later Bathsheba and Troy are on Yalbury Hill,
Troy having gambled on the races at Budmouth. They meet a woman

who is in a very poor condition. Troy dismounts and helps her. Bathsheba does not know who it is, but we learn that it is Fanny Robin. Troy arranges to meet her, and refuses to answer his wife's questions about her. Fanny goes on, and after an agonized journey, in which she is helped by a dog, she eventually reaches the Casterbridge Union, where she collapses. On that evening Troy borrows money from Bathsheba, who notices that he treasures a lock of hair in his watch-case. The next day, after Troy has gone to Casterbridge, there comes the news that Fanny Robin has died in the Union. Bathsheba's questions of Joseph Poorgrass and Liddy confirm her suspicions that the woman they met on the road was Fanny Robin, that Troy has treasured Fanny's lock of hair, and that he was Fanny's lover.

Troy is still away. Joseph Poorgrass goes to collect Fanny's body, which is to be brought back to Weatherbury. The atmosphere is oppressive with fog, and Joseph stops at an inn and drinks with Mark Clark and Jan Coggan. Gabriel arrives to reprimand him for the delay, and takes the coffin back himself. The funeral cannot take place that day, so the coffin is left at Bathsheba's overnight. Gabriel deletes '*and child*' from the chalk scrawl on the coffin in order to spare Bathsheba's feelings. Liddy, however, tells Bathsheba of the rumours. Bathsheba goes to see Gabriel, and from outside his house she sees him praying. She returns, looks in the coffin, and sees Fanny with the child. After praying herself, she is roused by the return of her husband, who is ignorant of what has happened. Troy kisses the dead Fanny, claims her as his real wife and treats Bathsheba with disdain. Bathsheba spends the night out of doors and is found by Liddy the next day. She determines to stick by her marriage for good or ill. Troy has a tomb erected to Fanny and surrounds it with flowers. Unfortunately the powerful streams from a gurgoyle wash away the flowers and cause watery havoc around the tomb. Troy is upset and sets forth on the Budmouth road. In the daylight Bathsheba and Gabriel contemplate the tomb.

Troy gets out of his depth when swimming off Budmouth, but is picked up by a brig. A report soon circulates that he is drowned, and Bathsheba is told at Casterbridge market. Bathsheba does not believe it, though a subsequent newspaper report and the arrival of Troy's clothes shake her intuitive disbelief. Boldwood takes hope from all this and renews his advances to Bathsheba, while Gabriel is not only made bailiff by Bathsheba, but is also given the superintendence of Boldwood's Lower Farm. Boldwood has the idea of waiting some six years until Bathsheba is free to marry. Troy then arrives, unknown to anybody, with the Greenhill Fair, at which he is performing as Dick Turpin. He sees Bathsheba, realizes that she may recognize his voice and cunningly mimes his part. He later finds that she is resting against him, unknown to herself, through the canvas of the tent. Bathsheba's ex-bailiff Pennyways hands her a note revealing that Troy is alive, but she delays reading it and Troy is able to steal it from her by slipping his hand under the bottom of the tent-cloth.

After this Boldwood rides home with her and again presses her to marry him some time in the future. She promises to consider the matter and to give him her answer by Christmas. She consults Gabriel, who is sympathetic towards Boldwood. Bathsheba is somewhat piqued that Gabriel does not express his love for her openly. On the night of the Christmas Eve party Bathsheba and Boldwood prepare for the occasion, Bathsheba confiding her thoughts to Liddy and Boldwood – now very dress-conscious – confiding his to Gabriel. Meanwhile Troy, who has employed Pennyways on his behalf, makes his own preparations for a dramatic entrance. He puts on a heavy grey overcoat with a cap, in order to disguise himself. The workmen gather outside Boldwood's house. Their talk is of Troy's being seen in the area, and they discuss whether Bathsheba should be told. They overhear Boldwood expressing his love for her. Laban Tall is deputed to tell Bathsheba the news, but he cannot get near her. Bathsheba, under pressure, agrees to marry Boldwood after six years, and the men wait broodingly near the door. A stranger is announced, who wishes to see Bathsheba. It is Troy, and he commands her to go with him. When he touches her, Boldwood shoots him dead. He tries to shoot himself, but Samway thwarts him, and Boldwood leaves the house.

Boldwood goes to the prison and gives himself up. Gabriel fetches a surgeon, but when they arrive Bathsheba has done all that is needful and prepared Troy for burial. Boldwood is tried and condemned to death. Many clothes and jewels, the preparations for his marriage, are found in his home, all labelled 'Bathsheba Boldwood'. Boldwood is reprieved and confined to prison (or an institution) for the rest of his life. Bathsheba gradually recovers. She has had Troy buried in the same grave as Fanny Robin. In the spring she learns that she is to lose

Gabriel; it is too much for her, and she goes to see him. Her manner convinces him that she loves him. They are married quietly, though the men come to visit them in the evening, before celebrating where they are happiest – at Warren's Malthouse.

An Account of the Plot

CHAPTER I, PP. 51-6

The opening description of Gabriel Oak is complemented by that of Bathsheba Everdene. This constitutes the reader's introduction to the two main characters of the novel, in which their basic characteristics are indicated. (See pp. 50 and 56 for what their names tell of their natures.) Gabriel's practical nature and his attention to detail and to time are particularized in the description of the watch. He is unassuming, modest and in his prime. Bathsheba shows her vanity by her obsession with the looking-glass, and her contemplation of herself (without visible audience) underlines this. She is, in Gabriel's eyes, 'a fair product of Nature in the feminine kind' (p. 55). Gabriel's behaviour at the turnpike-gate displays his judgement and speed of action, while Bathsheba's response shows her pride and how much she resents being crossed. Gabriel's assessment that her greatest fault is her vanity is fundamentally true. Her beauty, and her wish to have her beauty noticed, make her vulnerable. Throughout the chapter we are aware of the detail in the description, and the vivid, pictorial quality of the writing. The interaction between Bathsheba and Oak anticipates the many conflicts to come before their final love. The dialogue is clear, and the movement of the narrative keeps the reader expectant.

CHAPTER II, PP. 57-64

It is part of Hardy's insistent irony that the longest night should be filled with incident. The description of nature in this chapter, as elsewhere, is superb. Nature is personified in such phrases as 'a tongue of air' (p. 57) and the language is poetic; the 'wailing' of the trees is likened to 'the regular antiphonies of a cathedral choir' (p. 58). There is a desolate atmosphere and a fine sense of perspective in 'the roll of the world' (p. 58). Above all, there is a strongly particularized sense of place.

Oak, playing his flute, is seen at this stage as having a solitary existence. The account of him is brief and concise, indicating exactly what he possesses. A hint is given of the precariousness of his position, for his sheep are kept on 'a wild slope'. The description of the new-born lamb shows Gabriel's humane care, and also Hardy's detailed observation. The interior of the hut is warm with Gabriel's life of simplicity and survival. Hardy uses – as he does throughout the novel – telling, brief similes, as here where the ventilation holes are 'like the lights of a ship's cabin' (p. 61). Through the wonderful description of the sky and the stars Hardy sets the small events of man against the cosmic perspective. Gabriel shows how sensitive he is to the scene in its 'speaking loneliness'. His observation of Bathsheba and her aunt with the new-born calf shows that Gabriel and Bathsheba are close to nature in their sympathetic identification with it. Remember that Gabriel is spying, and note that there is some drama in the fact that they have not yet spoken to each other.

CHAPTER III, PP. 65–72

Gabriel takes advantage of Bathsheba's loss of her hat. He returns to the plantation, finds it and retains it. As he is about to return it, he observes Bathsheba indulging her athletic caprice when she 'dexterously dropped backwards flat upon the pony's back, her head over its tail, her feet against its shoulders, and her eyes to the sky' (p. 65). Natural images, for example 'like a bowed sapling', are used to emphasize the resilience and physical appeal of Bathsheba. After she has milked the cow, Gabriel decides to return the hat, though he finds himself 'amused, perhaps a little astonished' (p. 66) at the performance he has witnessed.

There is a further description of Bathsheba's attractions, and although she is self-conscious, she exercises good control, so that 'it was the man who blushed, the maid not at all' (p. 67). Yet she shows how vulnerable she is by blushing when she realizes that Oak has seen her antics, and she quickly leaves. This is an index to her sensitivity. She is also offended by what she feels is Gabriel's lack of tact. The incident, which brings about a change in their attitudes, is accompanied by fine atmospheric writing about the coldness, when 'the breath of the sleepers freezes to the sheets' (p. 69). Oak's carelessness – the result of his tiredness – leads to Bathsheba's saving him and to his falling completely in love with her. Bathsheba shows spirit, practicality and the capacity to tease. Gabriel displays sincerity, warm appreciation and a simplicity that cannot match her verbal ingenuity. Bathsheba has still not told him her name.

CHAPTER IV, PP. 73–82

Gabriel's reactions to Bathsheba are conveyed with light mockery through a comparison with fluctuations on the money-market, as he weighs his chances with her. His dread of not seeing her after the cow goes dry stimulates him towards a resolution. As Hardy observes 'Love is a possible strength in an actual weakness' (p. 74). Gabriel determines to propose and takes the lamb with him, having his dog George in attendance. Gabriel's preparations, even down to his acquisition from the plantation of 'a new walking-stick', are described with gentle humour. There is a subtle indication of his coming disappointment in the brief description of the day as having 'a summer face and a winter constitution' (p. 74), which seems to suggest the attitude of Bathsheba towards him. Again Oak crosses Bathsheba inadvertently, here because the presence of the innocent George disturbs her cat.

There is fine humour, and perhaps pathos too, in Mrs Hurst's boasting of Bathsheba's (non-existent) suitors, and some drama in Oak's departure, when the impetuous Bathsheba is moved to run after him. Brief images define her physical and emotional state: she is 'panting like a robin' and her face is 'like a peony petal before the sun dries off the dew' (p. 77). Although Bathsheba is honest and direct in her attempts to be fair to Gabriel, she is still teasing and flirting too, with her hand slipping suddenly from his 'like an eel'. Gabriel's dismay when she says that she is not going to marry him shows the simple sincerity of the man. Bathsheba is intent on spirited independence, which is ironic, in view of her inability to cope with the sophistications of Sergeant Troy. She says that she won't be 'thought men's property'. Oak's promise of what he will provide for her is pathetic. When she rejects him she sums herself up admirably in the words 'I shouldn't mind being a bride at a wedding, if I could be one without having a husband' (p. 80). Oak's passion is wonderfully conveyed when he says he will '*keep wanting you* till I die' (p. 80). We sense that Bathsheba knows that she needs taming. She speaks with 'luminous distinctness and common sense' (p. 81), but Gabriel's openness disconcerts her. They seem fated to be in conflict.

CHAPTER V, PP. 83–7

After Gabriel learns that Bathsheba has left, he begins to idealize her all the more. The imagery in which his passion is described – he 'felt the secret fusion of himself in Bathsheba to be burning with a finer flame' (p. 83) is sexual in tone. There follows a detailed description of the dog George (note Hardy's minute observation), with particular emphasis on his wisdom and judgement, which contrasts with the lack of both in his enthusiastic and misguided son. The incident with the sheep is graphic and tense, from Oak's awakening at the sound of the bell to the vivid and appropriate simile of the 'younger dog standing against the sky – dark and motionless as Napoleon at St Helena' (p. 86). The dog is as doomed as Napoleon, and he has caused Gabriel to lose his world. We are moved by Oak's compassion for his creatures and by his generous feelings in this terrible adversity: 'Thank God I am not married: what would *she* have done in the poverty now coming upon me!' (p. 86). Hardy uses death imagery to mirror the deaths of the sheep: 'the attenuated skeleton of a chrome-yellow moon' and 'The pool glittered like a dead man's eye' (p. 87). It leads to the wise, if cynical, statement that we live in 'a world made up so largely of compromise' (p. 87).

CHAPTER VI, PP. 88–97

This chapter marks the passage of time and re-creates the atmosphere and practice of the traditional hiring fair, with Gabriel, desperate in his need for work, changing from bailiff to shepherd in the hope of being taken on. There is a considered stress on the uncertainties of employment. Gabriel is at an initial disadvantage in having had his own farm, for he is thus considered to be a man marked by failure: 'Gabriel, like his dog, was too good to be trustworthy' (p. 89). Chance or Fate, always evident in Hardy's novels, alters his course, for he learns that there is a fair nearer Weatherbury, where Bathsheba has gone. Gabriel's journey gives Hardy the occasion for some fine description of nature and the countryside.

Gabriel falls asleep, which is predictable in view of his tiredness, and when he wakes (Hardy again describes his surroundings) he overhears a conversation about a vain woman between Billy Smallbury and Joseph Poorgrass. This part of the rustic group is acting as chorus to the main character, for Gabriel suddenly suspects that they are speaking of Bathsheba. Shortly after he leaves the waggon – note the element of chance once more – he sees the fire in the rick-yard. With singular presence of mind and admirable practicality, he supervises the fight against it. The description is vivid and immediate through its telling images: 'like melting sugar' and 'like the coal of a cigar' (p. 94). Gabriel gets his reward, for he finds, in a fine dramatic stroke at the end of the chapter, that the farmer he has saved is none other than Bathsheba. He shows his nerve – and a certain opportunist boldness – in humbly asking her if she wants a shepherd. Fate has brought them together again.

CHAPTER VII, PP. 98–101

Bathsheba's hesitancy is overcome by the rustic chorus in support of Gabriel, but her decision to refer Gabriel to the bailiff quickly breaks off anything personal between them. A subtle touch signifies the shiftiness of the bailiff as he moves 'past Oak as a Christian edges past an offertory-plate when he does not mean to contribute' (p. 99).

Oak's bewilderment at Bathsheba's sudden rise in the world causes Hardy to observe that 'some women only require an emergency to make them fit for one' (p. 99). Oak's encounter with the slim, thinly clad girl (later to be revealed as Fanny Robin) is dramatic. It reflects Gabriel's humanity and the natural compassion he shows to those in adversity, whether it be physical or emotional. The reader notes the irony in the girl's remarking to Gabriel that he is 'Only a shepherd – and you seem almost a farmer by your ways' (p. 100). Gabriel is moved by their meeting, and, after touching the girl's wrist, he senses her excitement and suffering.

CHAPTER VIII, PP. 102–20

A wonderful scene is now enacted. The interior of the malthouse is described in convincing detail, as are the idiosyncrasies of the occupants and their reactions to the presence of a stranger. The agricultural, working-class dialogue provides natural and essentially simple humour, which is obviously relished by the author. Note particularly his play on age when he applies the terms 'young' to a man of sixty-five and 'child' to one of forty. Typical of Hardy's writing is the sharply drawn picture of the God-forgive-me (p. 104). Gabriel naturally wishes to be accepted as one of the company. He propitiates them by saying, 'I never fuss about dirt in its pure state' (p. 105) and draws upon himself a compliment from the maltster as a result: 'his grandfer were just such a nice unparticular man!' (p. 105).

Each member of the group is whimsically, wittily but affectionately particularized. They have anecdotes, stories and, of course, news of Bathsheba. The most pathetic of the group is, perhaps, the bashful and blushing Joseph Poorgrass, who tells his own story of his attempts to cure himself, a tale that is capped by Jan Coggan's narrative of the poor unfortunate's response to an owl. Gabriel's question prompts the men to say what they know of Bathsheba. She is her uncle's heiress and has taken over the farm. This leads to further reminiscences from the group about her uncle and her parents. The maltster's account of Bathsheba's fickle father is both relevant and funny. The trap of marriage (which is later to close on Troy and Bathsheba), caused him to make his wife 'take off her wedding-ring' and make believe she was his sweetheart again. The criticism of the bailiff prepares the way for Gabriel to succeed him. The running banter between the rustics is enhanced by fine descriptive phrases, for example 'antithetic laughter'. The maltster tells his story at self-indulgent length, and is at first undermined and then pacified by the collective company. Gabriel, in obliging mood and mindful of being accepted, entertains on his flute. The focus shifts temporarily as the humour is directed at the newly married and henpecked Laban Tall.

The dramatic story of Bathsheba flying out at Pennyways for stealing the barley is followed by the announcement of further news – the report of Fanny Robin's disappearance, which causes Joseph Poorgrass to refer to the superstition 'I've seen a magpie all alone' (p. 117). The fact that Bathsheba initiates inquiries shows her sense of responsibility with regard to Fanny. Once more we are made aware of Gabriel's sensitivity as later that night his imagination moved 'like a river flowing rapidly under ice' (p. 119). There is little doubt that he is exceptional; his books and his knowledge of them indicate the quality of the man.

CHAPTER IX, PP. 121–6

Hardy's interest in and knowledge of architecture is abundantly clear from the opening of this chapter, in which Bathsheba's house is described in detail. Its incongruities are stressed and Hardy allows his lively imagination to play over it all, as may be seen in the picture of the stairs 'twisting round like a person trying to look over his shoulder' (p. 122). The narrative focuses on the character of Liddy and the special nature of her relationship to Bathsheba. There is a neat exchange between the two girls when they hear the knock on the door. The minor characters too are brought alive by Hardy's description of them. Boldwood's visit to inquire about Fanny Robin's disappearance is intriguing, since he is within reach, though not sight, of the fascination that is to deprive him of his sanity. Bathsheba shows her interest in the local gossip, and her questions about Boldwood indicate her impetuous and flirtatious tendencies. Master Coggan's reporting that Bathsheba is 'staid' irritates her. Again irony is present, for she is to be anything but staid with Boldwood. Bathsheba, aware of status, says that the man who proposed to her 'wasn't quite good enough for me' (p. 126). The chapter closes with a rather comic picture of the men filing in for their pay.

CHAPTER X, PP. 127–33

Bathsheba is practical, authoritative and generous. She is also direct, telling the men that the bailiff is dismissed, and sympathetically concerned over Fanny. The chapter provides interesting details throughout of the agricultural practices of the day. Bathsheba finds out all she can about her employees, whose responses are imbued with the natural humour and whimsicality they have shown at Warren's. Bathsheba demonstrates that she has her share of wit, saying to the stammering Andrew Randle, 'finish thanking me in a day or two'. (p. 129). Laban Tall's wife contributes to the humour through her dominating presence, referring to her husband as 'a poor gawkhammer mortal'. The conversation about the naming of Cain Ball shows, in its black comedy, Hardy's awareness of the ignorance present in some of the poor agricultural families. Gabriel is surprised at Bathsheba's coolness and air of authority. There follows the report of Fanny's going off with the soldiers, and Bathsheba's strong instruction to them not to suppose that 'because I'm a woman I don't understand the difference between bad goings-on and good' (p. 132). Her own exit is delightfully capped by Liddy's following her 'with a milder dignity not entirely free from travesty' (p. 133).

CHAPTER XI, PP. 134–8

This short chapter is dramatic and pathetic. It contains some appraisal of Troy and hints of his traits, and takes a closer look at the vulnerable and susceptible nature of Fanny Robin. There is a fine atmospheric description of the encroachment of winter, which brings darkness and depression, consonant with Fanny's state; wall, sky and river are each expressive of gloominess. Fanny's slightness of stature is given a morbid stress, too, almost as if she will be unequal to life. This adds to her pathos, which is enhanced by the feeble throwing of snow. The dialogue shows Fanny's anguish; her use of the word 'wife' expresses her poignant wish, which is never to become fact. Troy's distance from impetuous promises – 'I said that you might' (p. 137) – indicates the coolness of his response. He presents an immediate and effective contrast with Fanny, for he is casual and affects forgetfulness of what is vital to Fanny, the promise of marriage. There is a chilling deliberation in his response to Fanny's assertion that he had made many promises to marry her: 'If I said so, of course I will' (p. 138). The fact that the chapter ends in laughter is a further underlining of Troy's insensitivity. We feel strongly for Fanny and her situation, particularly when she says out of her injured innocence, 'There are bad women about, and they think me one' (p. 138).

CHAPTER XII, PP. 139–43

The farmers' gathering at the Corn Exchange is given light, humorous treatment, seen particularly in their use of the saplings. A series of brief images emphasizes the effect of Bathsheba's femininity on them. She is seen as 'a chaise between carts', 'as a romance after sermons' and 'like a breeze among furnaces' (p. 139). She has the confidence to follow the male conventions required and carries them through well, though Hardy refers to her as 'that lithe slip of humanity' (p. 140). She shows her firmness, and her impact is triumphant, but she becomes aware of the fact that one man seems to be unaware of her, namely Farmer Boldwood. This is certainly ironic in the light of his later capitulation. Boldwood's major outward quality is his dignity. Bathsheba's own reaction to her ordeal under the eyes of the male farmers is rather piquant, for she tells Liddy 'it was as bad as being married' (p. 142). She shows her capacity for romance by pondering on Boldwood's past sad love affair. This prepares us for her indulgence – casually but fatefully undertaken – in the next chapter.

CHAPTER XIII, PP. 144–8

The chapter heading 'Sortes Sanctorum', meaning holy fortune-telling, is ironic since Bathsheba's fortune-telling is undertaken light-heartedly on a Sunday in unholy surroundings and has unpredictable and disastrous results. Hardy's natural imagery is used in association with Liddy, who 'like a little brook, though shallow, was always rippling' (p. 144). The fortune-telling with the Bible and key is mentioned by Liddy and implemented by Bathsheba's impetuosity. When she turns to the Book of Ruth, Hardy sums up the situation epigrammatically by observing that 'It was Wisdom in the abstract facing Folly in the concrete' (p. 145). Liddy is cunning but seemingly casual in her provocation, for her report of Boldwood's indifference is what really makes Bathsheba decide to send him the valentine. Even here there is a strong element of chance, for she has to toss up to see whether the valentine should go to Boldwood or Teddy Coggan. The casualness – 'So very idly and unreflectingly was this deed done' (p. 148) – carries its terrible irony in the impact which the seal MARRY ME makes on the innocent and hitherto unaroused Boldwood.

CHAPTER XIV, PP. 149–52

The immediate effect of the valentine on Boldwood is conveyed with physical vividness as the seal appears 'as a blot of blood on the retina of his eye' (p. 149). Again Hardy employs an epigrammatic turn of phrase to depict the disturbing effect of the letter on Boldwood: 'the contemptibly little suggesting possibilities of the infinitely great' (p. 149). Boldwood's imaginative associations with the unknown writer of the valentine show that beneath his repressed and puritanical exterior he is a sensitive man. Unable to sleep, he gets up and watches the sunrise, described by means of comparison: 'The whole effect resembled a sunset as childhood resembles age' (p. 151). This is accompanied by Hardy's usual minute observation of nature. The chapter ends with a superbly visual set piece as Gabriel, on the skyline, moves the hurdles, and Boldwood, with the excuse of the letter addressed to Gabriel, goes towards him intent on finding out if he recognizes the handwriting of the valentine.

CHAPTER XV, PP. 153–63

Hardy's humour now encompasses the eating and drinking habits within the malthouse. The group once more acts as a kind of gossipy and evaluative chorus on the situation of Bathsheba. We learn that she is carrying on without a bailiff following the dismissal of Pennyways. They bemoan the situation and ponder on the various purchases she has made for the interior of the farmhouse. With the arrival of Gabriel and the lambs, the malthouse is used as a lambing-hut. The dialogue helps to create the wider background flavour of the period through such phrases as 'stirring times we live in' and 'how the face of nations alter' (p. 157).

Gabriel then becomes 'very warm' because he knows that the men have been discussing Bathsheba. He waxes angry, and the dog George growls in support. The rustics now seek to pacify Gabriel by dwelling on his cleverness. The idea of Oak's becoming bailiff is advanced, and Gabriel acknowledges that he had hoped that Bathsheba would appoint him. Just as the group becomes increasingly intent upon making Gabriel feel sorry for himself, Boldwood enters with what turns out to be Fanny Robin's letter. This dramatic and moving situation becomes ironic when Boldwood, after being shown the letter by Gabriel, expresses his fear that Fanny's confidence may be misplaced, for Troy has not yet married her, and goes on to give some account of Troy. His reservations here are more than borne out by subsequent events. When he finds out from Gabriel's identification of her handwriting that Bathsheba wrote the valentine and his speculation is over, the 'lonely and reserved man' is further tortured in his mind.

CHAPTER XVI, PP. 164-6

The narrative now turns logically to Fanny Robin following the dramatic and poignant import of her letter. In this effective scene, Troy is embarrassed and exposed to view in the church. The emphasis on the regularity of the striking jack, accompanied by the congregation's gigglings and fidgetings, creates the natural tension that is felt during a long, uncertain wait. The chuckling of the almsmen produces a grotesque atmosphere. The meeting between Troy and Fanny brings out their contrasting moods and attitudes, for she is abject and he is angry and humiliated. We get the impression that, despite the embarrassing circumstances, Troy is relieved at not being married, while Fanny is still desperate to be his wife.

CHAPTER XVII, PP. 167-9

The chapter opens with an account of the nature of Boldwood and his responses to the physicality of Bathsheba. He is so uncertain of his own judgement of her beauty that he seeks confirmation of it from a neighbour. Bathsheba is, of course, unaware of what she has done to Boldwood by sending him the valentine. Already he is jealous when she speaks to another man, sufficient indication of his passionate and unbalanced nature. Bathsheba realizes that she has triumphed with him, but regrets what she has done. She does not know how to put things right without humiliating or hurting him.

CHAPTER XVIII, PP. 170-74

Boldwood has an almost aristocratic status in the neighbourhood. His loneliness and the monastic style of his life are stressed – Hardy refers to him as 'the celibate', while the stables are his 'almonry and cloister'. The key to his character and subsequent behaviour is to be found in the phrase 'If an emotion possessed him at all, it ruled him'

(p. 171). He has no lightness, no frivolity, and is deadly serious. Bathsheba's unawareness of this 'hotbed of tropic intensity' is given in some extenuation of her behaviour. The arrival of early spring is described and its force is compared with town mechanization.

Although Boldwood's heart is insulated 'by reserve', he determines to approach Bathsheba in the meadow. The situation allows for some fine description of their surroundings – 'the ground was melodious with ripples' (p. 173) – and the procedure of trying to get the lamb to 'take'. There is an arresting interaction among the main characters when Boldwood appears, with his awareness that everybody is looking at him, Bathsheba's determination not to 'interrupt the steady flow of this man's life' (p. 174) and Gabriel's suspicion that she has been coquettish with the farmer. All this combines to provide fascinating insights into the consciousness of the individuals.

CHAPTER XIX, PP. 175–80

What is made apparent here is the difference between reality and idealization, as Boldwood has the freedom at least to indulge himself in thoughts about Bathsheba. A beautiful description of the water-meadow and the practice of sheep-washing follows. Boldwood arrives and finds Bathsheba 'in a new riding-habit – the most elegant she had ever worn' (p. 176). Despite Boldwood's reserve, Bathsheba has 'a consciousness that love was encircling her like a perfume' (p. 177). Boldwood's direct proposal is evidence of his concentrated passion, and that passion gives him a pathetic and moving dignity as he manages to articulate, 'I want you to let me say I love you again and again!' (p. 178). Bathsheba's honesty and her repentance are of no avail against Boldwood's fixed and fired determination to believe what he wants to believe. He asks Bathsheba to call her whimsical sending of the valentine 'a sort of prophetic instinct – the beginning of a feeling that you would like me' (p. 179). His 'deep-natured' appeal and her inward sympathy for him are equally moving; they are followed by the tensions of their dialogue, which gives him hope but not relief.

CHAPTER XX, PP. 181–6

Bathsheba muses about the desirability of marriage to Boldwood, but is disquieted at the prospect. She holds herself responsible for what has happened, for she has both a conscience and a degree of moral sensitivity. Her weakness lies in her impetuosity or, as Hardy rather pompously puts it, she was 'An Elizabeth in brain and a Mary Stuart in spirit' (p. 182). In a superb paragraph on the grinding of the shears, Hardy draws an analogy with war, which seems to anticipate the coming impact of Troy on this rustic community. By comparing Oak with Eros, Hardy associates him indelibly with love. We note how dependent Bathsheba is on Gabriel for the answers to her questions about Boldwood. There is a delightful incident when Gabriel has to grasp her hands for a practical purpose and holds on longer than necessary.

Bathsheba shows her pride and temper, for Gabriel's responses are honest and are not distinguished by tact. The outcome is that Bathsheba, in a fit of capriciousness, dismisses him, and Gabriel caps her week's notice with a request to leave at once. Yet beneath the warmth of the exchange we recognize Gabriel's unchanging love for her and we suspect, though Bathsheba is here ignorant of her own feelings, that she too cares for him despite herself. The deliberate emphasis on the parting – Gabriel leaves with 'placid dignity' – is enhanced by the biblical reference.

CHAPTER XXI, PP. 187–93

A crisis arises shortly after, when the sheep get into the clover, but even in this temperature of excitement we register the humorous portrayal of the individual rustics. The visual focus is on Bathsheba, who is angered at this disaster, in her 'rather dashing velvet dress, carefully put on before a glass' (p. 188). There is a certain poignant parallel between this scene and the one in which Gabriel loses his flock (Chapter V). Bathsheba's obdurate pride temporarily overcomes her compassion, while her employees contribute their mite of conscious blackmail by naming Gabriel as the only person who can cure the sheep. The drama in Bathsheba's mind (and heart) is heightened by the grotesquely spectacular death of the ewe. Tension is present in the sequence of journey–return–journey–return, with the monotony and delay acting on Bathsheba's fevered imagination as well as the reader's.

The scene is now imbued with visual drama and the crisis of decision. Bathsheba's emotion is seen in her tears. Her note to Gabriel and its final words reveal her heart; the moving sincerity here should be compared with her thoughtlessly sending the valentine to Boldwood. The operations carried out by Gabriel are explained with graphic intensity. At the end of the chapter, with its themes of reconciliation and unvoiced love, the 'love-led man' is moved to return. Bathsheba still rules, unaware of her own deeper feelings for Gabriel, yet acknowledging her dependence upon him.

CHAPTER XXII, PP. 194–204

The picture of the countryside on the first day of June is richly painted with imaginative imagery, as in the likening of the cuckoo-pint to 'an apoplectic saint in a niche of malachite' (p. 194). The resemblance of the great barn to 'a church with transepts' invests the the sheep-shearing both with a ritualistic and an ancient quality. The description of the barn and its traditional associations is given with warmth, something close to love. This solid and unswerving respect for tradition causes Hardy to note that the bar has 'a satisfied sense of functional continuity' (p. 195) as he contemplates it. The permanence of the country ways of life as against the changes of the town is Hardy's moral theme; the scene has a timelessness, which the writer strives to record.

Meanwhile, Gabriel luxuriates in being under Bathsheba's eyes. There is an unvoiced but telling connection between the sheep that blushes and Bathsheba, almost as if she herself fears exposure of her feelings and susceptibilities. Gabriel displays his expertise at the shearing. The initialling of the sheep is described in the present tense to bring the scene more vividly and immediately to the reader. The sudden appearance of Boldwood is a dramatic stroke, but our feelings are with Gabriel, particularly when he is reprimanded by Bathsheba for cutting a sheep. His carelessness is due only to his concern for her, which makes him try to watch Boldwood. Rustic gossip about them attends the departure of Boldwood and Bathsheba.

Henery Fray's wish to be bailiff and his understated language provide comic relief, though Gabriel rises to the bait in defence of Bathsheba, and the maltster in turn has to be pacified. Gabriel remains depressed at the thought that Bathsheba will have Boldwood. There is every indication that the shearing-supper will bring events to a head, though the rustics are merely filled with happy expectation.

CHAPTER XXIII, PP. 205–11

The seating arrangements at the shearing-supper are very significant: Bathsheba is part and yet not part of the company, and Gabriel sits in the prominent helping position until displaced by Boldwood, as in life. Coggan's song is ironically pertinent to Gabriel's state, and Joseph Poorgrass's song has its relevance too. It is attended by his own diffidence, promoted by the encouragement of others, while the scarcely concealed laughter of young Bob Coggan puts an end to it. Hardy uses some ominous images as a prelude to crisis – 'The sun had crept round the tree as a last effort before death' (p. 207), which has the effect of making the atmosphere uncertain despite the outward celebration. The classical analogies with Silenus and Homer's gods again stress the timelessness, the recurrent nature of what is happening.

Hardy's attention to structural detail is shown when Bathsheba sings 'The Banks of Allan Water'. The verse quoted anticipates Troy's later courtship of her, and it is long remembered 'by more than one of those who were gathered there' (p. 208). Oak watches Boldwood and reads all the signs of his love. There is some humorous mockery of Pennyways (who is present despite having been sacked), for his failure to steal anything from the supper. The happiness of the company contrasts with the passionate scene in the parlour between

Boldwood and Bathsheba. Hardy quotes from Keats's 'Ode to a Nightingale' to define Boldwood's happiness in hope (though the ode is in fact redolent of death), and from Thomas Gray's 'Ode on a Distant Prospect of Eton College' to describe Bathsheba's mixed feelings at the situation in which she finds herself.

CHAPTER XXIV, PP. 212–18

Gabriel shows his love and his constancy in checking up on Bathsheba's property, a nightly display of loyalty of which Bathsheba knows nothing. Hardy's narrative focuses on the sounds of the night, and he affectionately tells how the breathings of the Devon cows obtrude upon the silence.

This is followed by a fine atmospheric description of the fir plantation through which Bathsheba proceeds, 'the plumy ceiling of which was supported by slender pillars of living wood' (p. 213). The place and its darkness, together with the trapping of Bathsheba's skirt (anticipating her being trapped into love by Troy), generate strong dramatic tension. The word 'hooked' is particularly prophetic of the future relationship between Bathsheba and Troy. We note immediately the opportunism of Troy, and there is a strong sexual atmosphere about the encounter. The grotesque distortion of their outlines in shadow, which somehow heightens the unreality of the experience, also hints at a distortion to come. Hardy's appropriate imagery – the gathers of the dress give way 'like lilliputian musketry' – and the emphasis on Bathsheba's responses and apprehensions underline how easily Troy dominates her and how Bathsheba is unable to contain him here, as later. Troy is superbly adaptable, knowing what to say: he calls her 'beautiful'. He even unconsciously, and shallowly anticipates the future: 'I wish it had been the knot of knots, which there's no untying!' (p. 216).

Bathsheba's impressionability is seen in her reception of Liddy's words on Troy – 'gay' and 'a clever young dand' (p. 217) – and on his forebears. The conclusion of the chapter shows how successful Troy has been with Bathsheba.

CHAPTER XXV, PP. 219–22

The character of Troy is presented and investigated. It is summed up in the finely economical 'With him the past was yesterday: the future, to-morrow: never, the day after' (p. 219). Hardy's own commentary on Troy's nature is philosophical, though somewhat laboured. Troy indulges his own tendencies, particularly his amorous ones. He is dependent on chance, responding to what happens at the time. He is well educated, fluent, natural, spontaneous and capable of turning any situation to his own advantage. His sexual attitudes and morality are summed up in his observation with regard to women: 'Treat them fairly, and you are a lost man' (p. 221). Hardy ironically refers to him as 'This philosopher'. His opportunism is seen in his undertaking the haymaking with the intention of seeing Bathsheba, which he does.

CHAPTER XXVI, PP. 223–32

The interaction between Troy and Bathsheba shows his fluency, his natural facility for flattery, and her defensiveness. Troy easily gets the better of the exchanges – he is adept at this kind of thing through long practice – and he turns the conversation to his own advantage with natural verve. His remark about curses and kisses renders Bathsheba speechless. She recognizes his sly ability and tries to hide her 'dimplings of merriment'. Bathsheba is flattered and shows her susceptibility to his attentions by wanting to hear more. In Hardy's word, this is 'Capitulation', and Troy is now certain that he is going to succeed with her. She unwittingly shows him her pleasure after he has spelled out – at length – the fatal nature of her attractions. Troy further draws out her emotional concern by telling her that he will be going away shortly. Such is the speed with which he improves his position that he is soon able to assert with all the appearance of sincerity 'I loved you then, at once – as I do now' (p. 229). The offer of the watch, a fine piece of opportunism, is calculated to move Bathsheba both momentarily and deeply; the impact of the motto is almost as strong as the gift itself. Bathsheba is overcome, wondering how much of what Troy asserts is true. Although the reader suspects Troy of being shallow, there is no doubting his dexterity and charm; perhaps he may even be credited with a passing sincerity.

CHAPTER XXVII, PP. 233–6

The opening description of the habits of the bees again shows Hardy's close and loving observation of nature. Bathsheba reveals both courage and a temporary independence in seeking to hive the bees herself. There is something unconsciously humorous in her undignified sliding down the ladder. Bathsheba's behaviour and insistence that Troy is protected with the hat and veil indicate that she is already deeply in love with him. Her laughter, observes Hardy, 'was the removal of yet another stake from the palisade of cold manners which had kept him off' (p. 234). The strongly charged sexual atmosphere is enhanced by the reference to the sword-exercise and the assignation to see it, which signals Bathsheba's complete succumbing to Troy.

CHAPTER XXVIII, PP. 237–42

Bathsheba's indecision, followed by her retreat and return, show her state of mind. The aura of the scene with the sword-exercise – the thrusts, the expertise, the fear – speaks of sexual compulsion as exercised by Troy over Bathsheba. Troy's 'sleight of hand' suggests seduction, while a sequence of images conveys the immediacy of the experience that Bathsheba undergoes. The cutting of the lock of hair, with its strongly physical overtone, shows the extent of Troy's power over Bathsheba, while the killing of the caterpillar on Bathsheba's bosom generates sexual tension. Bathsheba 'felt powerless to withstand or deny him' (p. 241). His kiss is majestically the kiss of mastery.

CHAPTER XXIX, PP. 243–50

Bathsheba has now given herself over completely to love of Troy, and her 'Weakness is doubly weak by being new' (p. 243). The authorial voice makes a telling contrast between Troy and Oak, for while the former's 'deformities lay deep down from a woman's vision', Oak's 'virtues were as metals in a mine' (p. 244). Gabriel has registered Bathsheba's behaviour and suffers accordingly. He believes that she is making a snare for herself.

He has the boldness and directness to approach her, but when he has contrived the meeting he finds words difficult. He offends her by suggesting that since Boldwood can't meet her, he, Oak, has come to safeguard her instead. Bathsheba is stung enough to tell him that she has no intention of marrying Boldwood, and Gabriel's response is to warn her bluntly about Troy. When Oak says 'I believe him to have no conscience at all' (p. 246), we marvel at his lack of wisdom, since this is bound to provoke Bathsheba. Oak elaborates, and Bathsheba's ensnaring by Troy is evident in the image 'No Christmas robin detained by a window-pane ever pulsed as did Bathsheba now' (p. 247). Troy's deception over his supposed entry to the church 'by the old tower door' (p. 247) is an indication of his opportunist and wayward character. Gabriel makes a moving assertion of his own love for Bathsheba, and there is a quiet and self-effacing dignity in what Hardy calls Oak's 'grim fidelity' (p. 249). Oak suffers when he suspects that Bathsheba has deceived him and that she has really come there to meet Troy.

CHAPTER XXX, PP. 251–5

Bathsheba's reactions show just how completely dominated she is by thoughts of Troy, while the brief phrase 'so he stated' suggests that Troy may be deceiving her. We learn that she had forbidden him to meet her that evening, but had been unable to keep to her decision, and had turned up herself. Letters play an important part in this novel. Bathsheba now writes her rejection to Boldwood, and the letter stands in contrast to her earlier invitation by valentine. When Bath-sheba overhears Liddy and the servants talking about her – and their dialogue is somewhat prophetic – she realizes how much her affairs are a focus of gossip. The vacillations of her mood are shown in her conversations with the servants, for she is torn this way and that by her feelings. Her confession to Liddy reveals impassioned anguish rather than happiness: 'I love him to very distraction and misery and agony!' (p. 253). She is literally begging for reassurance about Troy from Liddy, but rages at her so much that Liddy wishes to leave her. As a result, Bathsheba drops from 'haughtiness to entreaty with capricious inconsequence' (p. 254). Their reconciliation is both humor-ous and pathetic, the two women bound to one another by the shared secret of Bathsheba's agonized love for Troy.

CHAPTER XXXI, PP. 256–64

Bathsheba determines to accompany Liddy on a visit in order to keep out of Boldwood's way, but on her walk she meets Boldwood, who is 'stunned and sluggish now'. His former reasoning that she would accept him 'now came back as sorry gleams from a broken mirror' (p. 257). Bathsheba is embarrassed. Boldwood's emotions have been 'paralysed by her letter'. She feels that his terrible look cannot be answered in words, and her suffering becomes intolerable as he tries to get her to change her mind. He begs her to have pity on him and, with unconscious irony, uses the word 'mad' to define his own state. What he calls 'encouragement', she calls 'the childish game of an idle minute' (p. 259), which conveys the extent of their real distance from each other.

The ensuing exchange is underpinned by the irony that Boldwood has yet to reveal that he knows that Troy has entered Bathsheba's life. He becomes progressively more bitter, saying 'Would to God you had never taken me up, since it was only to throw me down!' (p. 260). The pathos deepens as Boldwood asks Bathsheba to say she 'only wrote that refusal to me in fun' (p. 260). His bitterness now expends itself on Troy, and we note that part of his suffering is because of his loss of face in the area. As their exchanges become unbearable in their intensity, so Hardy observes 'The most tragic woman is cowed by a tragic man' (p. 262). Boldwood's rage at Troy takes on a passionately prophetic note: 'a time of his life shall come when he will have to repent' (p. 262). Bathsheba is terrified that he will carry out his threats against Troy and is amazed at discovering 'Such astounding wells of fevered feeling in a still man' (p. 263). The depths of Bathsheba's sensitivity and love are exposed in these fears.

CHAPTER XXXII, PP. 265–73

An atmosphere of tension is created at Weatherbury in the night. The excitement generated by what Maryann sees is increased with the rousing of Gabriel to follow the stolen horse and the pursuit is graphically described. By borrowing Boldwood's horses Gabriel shows his initiative and practical approach. The tracking by the pursuers sustains the excitement, as the identity of the horse they are following, but not its rider, becomes clear. The fact that it has become lame heightens the tension, for they know they will catch up soon. When they overtake at the turnpike-gate there is a superb unexpectedness in the discovery that they have been tracking Bathsheba all the time. Her exchange with Gabriel and Coggan is at first testy. An element of chance has played a part in their not having seen the message she left on the coach-house doors. Bathsheba is made all the more sensitive because Gabriel and Coggan have used Boldwood's horses, but she appreciates their loyalty to her, embarrassing though it now is. Gabriel enjoins secrecy upon Coggan.

Bathsheba has deluded herself that she can give up Troy. She knows the truth about him, but cannot help herself. By going to him in this way she is yielding to temptation; she is not asserting her will but showing that she is in effect completely in his power.

CHAPTER XXXIII, PP. 274–81

Bathsheba's stay in Bath rouses suspicions. Meanwhile, the harvesting begins and the work in the fields is described in detailed atmospheric writing. Superstition rules Maryann, who breaks a key and considers it 'a dreadful bodement'. There is the now customary give-and-take of the men's humour as the group awaits the arrival of Cain Ball. He commands attention at once when he speaks of Bath, though his choking makes for a mixture of comedy and irritation, the latter primarily on the part of the apprehensive Gabriel. Gradually Cainy gets out his story of Bathsheba and Troy, so far as it goes. The humour continues in Cain's being dosed with cider and in Joseph Poorgrass's account of his own diffidence. These delays suggest that there is still more news to come about Bathsheba and Troy. Whatever is said about them causes Gabriel acute suffering. He has difficulty in getting any information, for his companions proceed to evaluate what they consider life in Bath is like. Cainy is determined to complete his recital, though there is no more to tell except how he adapted himself to the different religious observances required at the time. Although Gabriel is very dispirited, the comic exchanges among the rustics, which run throughout the chapter, set the mood.

CHAPTER XXXIV, PP. 282–92

Gabriel observes Bathsheba's return and is made aware of her listless mood. He himself experiences a sense of relief that she is back. The description of the timid hares is followed by the dramatic passing of Boldwood, another lonely nocturnal wanderer. His wish to apologize to Bathsheba shows how determinedly he has striven to overcome his unreasoning passion. When Liddy tells him that Bathsheba cannot see him, he feels the rejection keenly and is humiliated at not even having the chance to be forgiven. But before there is much time for thought, Troy arrives.

Boldwood accosts Troy when he finds that he is going to call on Bathsheba and attempts to buy him off. When Boldwood tells him he ought to marry Fanny Robin, Troy says cryptically, 'Indeed, I wish

to, but I cannot' (p. 284). As we learn later, there is an underlying
irony in this exchange, since Troy has already married Bathsheba,
and it renders Boldwood's pleas and attempts to bribe Troy all the
more pathetic. Troy dupes him by accepting the offers, thus showing
what a cold-hearted trickster he is. At last Boldwood detects the
mockery in his tormentor's tone, and he then overhears the intimacy
of the words between Troy and Bathsheba. After Bathsheba leaves,
the enraged Boldwood attacks Troy, and is only restrained by Troy's
telling him 'You are injuring her you love!' (p. 288). Troy heartlessly
suggests that Boldwood would be better off killing himself. Boldwood, at the whim of his emotional instability, now begs Troy to
marry Bathsheba, because he feels that this is the only way to secure
her happiness. Such is his new obsession that he now wishes to settle
money on Bathsheba if Troy marries her. Boldwood's humiliation
and anguish are compounded when he reads of Troy's marriage to
Bathsheba. Boldwood is almost demented.

CHAPTER XXXV, PP. 293–6

The 'time of sun and dew' (p. 293) is minutely described. With Troy's
appearance in the window, Coggan immediately knows the truth.
Gabriel has to come to terms with it too, and Coggan tells him 'you
look like a corpse!' (p. 294). Gabriel has a distinctly prophetic insight,
looking ahead to 'the scenes of repentance that would ensue from this
work of haste' (p. 294). He is both grief-stricken and amazed. Troy is
already adopting the attitude of the new proprietor, coming into
reflex conflict with Gabriel about the nature of the house, a difference
that perhaps reflects their different morality too. Troy makes an
apparently casual remark about the possibility of insanity in Boldwood's family, but because of Boldwood's extremities of passion, it
lodges in the reader's mind. Gabriel's pride is offended by Troy's
throwing the half-crown. When Boldwood appears, Gabriel is moved
by the stricken immobility of the man, which takes on tragic proportions: 'as in laughter there are more dreadful phases than in tears, so
was there in the steadiness of this agonized man an expression deeper
than a cry' (p. 296).

CHAPTER XXXVI, PP. 297–305

The sinister aspect of the night, with the motionless man 'looking at the moon and sky' (p. 297), create a tense atmosphere. All is redolent of an approaching thunderstorm. Meanwhile, the celebration of Troy and Bathsheba proceeds, and only Oak is mindful of the exposed ricks outside. Troy is 'lolling' beside Bathsheba in a manner indicative of his casual and irresponsible attitude now that he is married. After the dance to 'The Soldier's Joy' (its appropriateness is commented on), Gabriel's fears are dismissed by Troy, who believes that it will not rain. Troy is intent on making the men drunk by mixing their drinks, much to Bathsheba's annoyance. Already the differences between them are apparent. When Oak leaves, the presence of the toad, which felt 'like a boxing-glove', is the first of a number of presages in nature of the coming storm. There is a superb description of the behaviour of the sheep. With great presence of mind, Gabriel acts to save the ricks. The picture of the drunken and sleeping men, and Gabriel's reaction to what it means for Bathsheba's marriage and livelihood, shows that he is still completely enamoured of her and ready to display his devotion and responsibility. The chapter ends in eerie darkness and silence before the storm.

CHAPTER XXXVII, PP. 306–12

The beginnings of the storm are conveyed through vivid imagery: 'like a mailed army', 'distinct as in a line engraving' and 'like an ink stroke on burnished tin' (p. 306). Gabriel extemporizes a lightning-conductor in his precarious position on the stack. At this moment Bathsheba appears and reveals that Troy had promised to safeguard the ricks. She helps Gabriel, though the atmosphere is frightening and the sound of the thunder is 'diabolical'. The storm is most vividly described; the lightning, noise and shadows seem to be per-forming a 'dance of death'. The lightning strike has a terrible inten-sity, and it gives Gabriel the trembling of Bathsheba's warm arm in his hand. She confides to Gabriel that, having gone to Bath to break off her engagement, she soon realized that scandal might attach itself to her; she married Troy because of that and because she feared his preference for another. This leaves Gabriel to ponder on 'the contradictoriness of that feminine heart' (p. 312).

CHAPTER XXXVIII, PP. 313–16

The effects of the driving storm upon the striving Gabriel are now made clear. He himself notes the irony of the fact that eight months previously he had been fighting fire in this very spot, and now he is combating the effects of rain out of his love for the same woman. The irresponsibility of the rest of the men is symbolized by the procession as they emerge from the barn with their hang-overs, led by the whistling and still jaunty Troy. Boldwood's arrival seems a complete contrast. Gabriel is amazed to find that – obviously because of his obsession with Bathsheba – he has left his ricks uncovered. Gabriel is struck by the coincidence of two neighbouring farmers taking the same risk, for although the reasons are different, the connection between them is striking. It is almost as if they have unwittingly brought it on each other. Boldwood is so overwrought by his love that he confides in Gabriel, finishing with 'a carelessness which was like the smile on the countenance of a skull' (p. 316).

CHAPTER XXXIX, PP. 317–21

The state of the relationship between Bathsheba and Troy is spelled out here: Bathsheba is listless and Troy is complaining at having lost money. Troy has indulged in gambling, to add to his other vices. His power is seen in the way he reprimands Bathsheba for her lack of pluck, though her objections stem from her sense of moral responsibility. He has grown contemptuous of her. The meeting with Fanny Robin is both dramatic and moving. Troy shows some compassion, but he hurriedly gets rid of Fanny because of Bathsheba's proximity. He arranges to meet her, returns to the gig, and whips the horses, refusing to name the girl to Bathsheba. She is bruised emotionally by the meeting and by Troy's devil-may-care attitude towards her.

CHAPTER XL, PP. 322–8

Fanny's journey, in her isolation, is imbued with deep pathos, the darkness and the distant 'halo' above Casterbridge contributing to the hopelessness of her mood. The detail of the description of Fanny's face – 'young in the ground-work, old in the finish' (p. 322) – is reflected in the faces of the milestones whose marks she can only feel. The fashioning of the rough crutch is a measure of her determination, but her weakness is soon apparent. The imminence of her death is subtly indicated by Hardy in the clear sound of the fox's bark, 'its three hollow notes being rendered at intervals of a minute with the precision of a funeral bell' (p. 324). The anguish of the journey is seen in the description of her physical movements, the mental calculations, and the monologue, which keeps her going. The appearance of the dog, like the meeting with Troy and Bathsheba, suggests that Fate has come to her assistance. In a delusory way it has. The dog not only understands, but becomes frantic when it cannot do enough for her. The implicit comparison with the inadequacy of man, and the criticism of the failure of one in particular to do anything, are reinforced by the cruelty of stoning the dog away. The shelter of the Casterbridge Union is also delusory, and Hardy's imagery is conflicting: 'as the shape of a body is visible under a winding-sheet' and 'the place looked like an abbey' (p. 327).

CHAPTER XLI, PP. 329–39

Bathsheba and Troy have grown apart, and the gambling needs of Troy come before the wife who seeks pathetically to exert her fascination. In this case, however, Troy needs the money for Fanny, though Bathsheba does not know this. Troy's lies are easily exposed, but because of his arrogant attitude, this does not help Bathsheba.

There is irony in Troy's belief that Fanny is still living and in his saying 'women will be the death of me!' (p. 332), which, indirectly at least, is to prove true. Bathsheba's jealousy over the lock of hair reaches fever-point, and her distress is shown in her behaviour after Troy has gone out: 'She chafed to and fro in rebelliousness, like a caged leopard' (p. 333). Perhaps the most terrible aspect of Bathsheba's suffering is her feeling that she has degraded herself.

She sees Gabriel and Boldwood meet the next day, but not until Joseph Poorgrass comes to her does she learn what they were talking about, namely the death of Fanny Robin. Poorgrass's account – 'and 'a went like a candle-snoff' (p. 335) – indicates Fanny's weakness. Bathsheba immediately asserts that she, not Boldwood, will bring Fanny back. It is a pathetic mark of her enforced subservience in her marriage to Troy. Bathsheba generously proposes to strew her coffin with flowers, in a manner reminiscent of Ophelia in *Hamlet*. Her conversation with Poorgrass shows her that Fanny was the woman she met on the road with Troy and that the lock of yellow hair was hers. She further questions Liddy and, when the latter tells her that Troy said of Fanny's young man that he knew him 'as well as he knew himself' (p. 339), Bathsheba knows the truth in her heart.

CHAPTER XLII, PP. 340–51

The funereal atmosphere, somewhat eerie, is created by the focus on the matter-of-fact treatment of the coffin. The fog takes on a symbolic force as it encloses the driver and the waggon, and vivid phrases define the effect, as in 'The air was as an eye suddenly struck blind' (p. 341). In the wood Poorgrass feels his extreme isolation, but he changes when he reaches the inn and meets his old friends Jan Coggan and Mark Clark, 'owners of the two most appreciative throats in the neighbourhood' (p. 343). Poorgrass's drinking has to be curtailed so that he can resume his journey, though he stays on for more. Jan Coggan moralizes on the fact that too much drink 'leads us to that horned man in the smoky house' (p. 344), but claims they should make the most of their talent. Joseph is persuaded to stay on yet again, and the inherent humour of the scene contrasts strongly with the sombre picture of the dead Fanny in the coffin outside. There is more humour in their discussion of Church of England and Chapel. Again Joseph is persuaded to stay, but Oak arrives to reprimand him. Clark and Coggan reason that nothing more can be done for Fanny and Coggan's song reflects the rustic mood. The state of intoxication of Joseph Poorgrass is evident from his 'multiplying eye' (p. 347). He finds his tongue in a kind of maudlin self-pity.

Gabriel, as usual, takes over, since none of the others is fit to drive the waggon, and he goes to the manor-house. It is too late for the funeral that day, and it is put off until the next. Bathsheba's sensitivity and Christian feeling is such that she had the coffin brought into the house. Gabriel is deeply disturbed, fearing that Bathsheba will discover the truth. He remains with the body for some time, and, in his attempt to protect the woman he loves from greater suffering, he rubs out the words '*and child*' so that Bathsheba will not know of Troy's sin.

CHAPTER XLIII, PP. 352–61

The nervous state of Bathsheba is conveyed in her conversation with Liddy, and once more we are aware that she is asking for reassurance. She is divided against herself in her brooding and almost tries to be uncharitable towards Fanny (though in fact she cannot be) because Fanny preceded her with Troy. When Liddy returns with the rumour about Fanny, Bathsheba is distressed further. She has inklings of the truth and some suspicions because of the meeting on the road.

Such is Bathsheba's dependence on him now that she longs to ask Gabriel what he knows. With her usual impetuosity she leaves the house to go to him, but when she gets there she loses her nerve and cannot bring herself to knock. Her striking independence, though, reasserts itself when she gets back home. With characteristic courage she opens the coffin and sees 'the unconscious pair' and Fanny's face 'framed in by that yellow hair of hers' (p. 357). Her emotions are in a tumult after this. When she resolves to pray not to kill herself, we note that the sight of Gabriel praying has moved her to this. Soothed, she places flowers around Fanny's head.

The passing of time brings an unknowing Troy who, once he discovers that Fanny is dead, sinks forward to kiss her. This provokes Bathsheba to the assertion of her (albeit degraded) wifehood, and her pleas for a kiss are impassioned to the point of hysteria. Troy is bewildered at seeing his proud wife reduced in this way, but his response to the appeal is to claim Fanny as his true wife in the eyes of Heaven. His rejection of Bathsheba – 'You are nothing to me' (p. 361) – shows his cruel and selfish nature.

CHAPTER XLIV, PP. 362–8

Such is Bathsheba's shame that she runs out of the house and hides. There is a brilliant focus on the sounds of the birds and of the ploughboy. This in turn is followed by minute and fine description of Bathsheba's surroundings, particularly the swamp, which, in its poisonous malignity, acts as an equivalent to Bathsheba's state and her degraded life. She recovers sufficiently to be 'faintly amused' at the passing schoolboy's attempts at learning.

When Liddy appears, she is a great comfort to Bathsheba, who sensitively decides to stay outside until Fanny has been taken away. Liddy in fact oversees everything, having implied that Bathsheba is in her room and unwell. Bathsheba has resolved to face up to her marriage regardless of the cost to herself. With typical impetuosity she tells Liddy that she'd like to read some books, and then is moved to humour by choosing some titles that echo her own situation, for example Congreve's *The Mourning Bride*. Even in this adversity, Bathsheba has the spirit to be able to smile. The game played by the village lads shows that life goes on, but the erection of the ornate tombstone suggests that Bathsheba has yet more to endure.

CHAPTER XLV, PP. 369–73

This opens with a retrospect on Troy's actions when he went to meet Fanny before he knew of her death. He waits for her and when she does not arrive (she is, in fact, being laid out for burial at that time),

Troy becomes angry, remembering the earlier occasion when this had happened. He drives to the races in an angry and reckless mood, but some slight stir of conscience prevents him from gambling. The narrative then reaches the point where Troy awakes the morning after the scene with Bathsheba. Completely indifferent to Bathsheba's whereabouts and impetuously romantic, he goes to Casterbridge and has a tomb made for Fanny, spending all the money he has got. He works by night, grotesquely, irrationally, surrounding Fanny's grave with a variety of flowers. It is an echo, but distorted, of Bathsheba's own reaction to the dead Fanny. Both were showing their respect for the dead, but in Troy's case there is also motivation from his romantic and now idealized love.

CHAPTER XLVI, PP. 374–81

The picture of the gurgoyle sustains the grotesque atmosphere. The detail is enhanced by deliberate personification, for instance where Hardy observes that 'the creature had for four hundred years laughed at the surrounding landscape, voicelessly in dry weather, and in wet with a gurgling and snorting sound' (p. 375). The style here is vivid in its description of both sight and sound. The 'torrent from the gurgoyle's jaws' (p. 375) disturbs Fanny's grave. The washing out of the flowers symbolizes Troy's failure to provide for Fanny in death as in life. It is as if Fate has acted against Troy. The incident moves him greatly, so much so that this egoistic man feels, temporarily, a hatred for himself. He determines to leave.

Bathsheba, having imprisoned herself in the attic, learns from Liddy of the heavy rain and of Gabriel's friendly call. She also learns that Troy has gone to Budmouth. Then, in a duplication of the scene in which she and Troy stood on each side of Fanny's coffin, she and Gabriel stand on each side of her grave. They read Troy's inscription; Bathsheba conceals her feelings and, with singular resolution and sympathy, she re-plants the flowers.

CHAPTER XLVII, PP. 382–4

The depression and reactions of Troy are made known. He contemplates the sea, finds a small protected basin of it and decides to bathe. He is carried out to sea by the current and gets into difficulties, but he is picked up by a boat and the men promise to put him ashore the next day. There is a vivid description of the lights coming on in Budmouth as night falls. This short chapter is important in terms of the plot, for it moves the narrative forward to the results attendant upon Troy's supposed death.

CHAPTER XLVIII, PP. 385–9

The state of Bathsheba's mind and emotions, which may be compared with Troy's in the previous chapter, is described. She is now fatalistic in her acceptance of her husband. She is also practical and realizes that the precariousness of her position with regard to the farm means that she may have to face poverty. The announcement to her of Troy's drowning is dramatic and, in view of what the reader knows, ironic. By chance – a reflex of Fate – Boldwood is on hand to assist her, and despite his stiffness and gloom we note his tenderness to her when he smoothes her dress 'as a child might have taken a storm-beaten bird and arranged its ruffled plumes' (p. 387). Boldwood luxuriates in the memory of having her in his arms.

When Bathsheba arrives home we note that her insistent intuition rules her: she is convinced that Troy is alive. Her belief is undermined by the eyewitness's testimony and by the arrival of the clothes. There is a moving moment when, in a typically impetuous vein despite her adversity, Bathsheba decides to keep the lock of Fanny's hair. In a finely economic phrase Hardy calls the lock 'the fuse to this great explosion' (p. 389).

CHAPTER XLIX, PP. 390–95

Bathsheba's acceptance is evident from her 'mood of quietude which was not precisely peacefulness' (p. 390). She thinks much about the past and attends in a desultory way to the business of the farm. Oak becomes bailiff, and Boldwood – his dead crops expressive of his one-time death wish – also gives him responsibility for his farm, despite Bathsheba's initial half-hearted objections. As Hardy puts it, 'Gabriel's malignant star was assuredly setting fast' (p. 391). Oak's arrangement with Boldwood includes a share of the profits, and his independence is shown in his ignoring public opinion and continuing to live in his old way.

Meanwhile, hope has 'germinated' again in Boldwood, whose devotion to Bathsheba is described as a 'fond madness'. He proposes to use a much more common-sense approach to Bathsheba and to this end he questions Liddy about her mistress. Even as he talks, however, we notice his emotional temperature, his feelings ever rising and falling from hope to misery. Such is his conscience that he considers he has been underhand in sounding out Liddy. He focuses on the idea that Bathsheba might marry him after the passage of six years, thus giving unwonted weight to what Liddy has said. Expectation is aroused at the end of the chapter by the mention of the arrival of the Greenhill Fair.

CHAPTER L, PP. 396–409

The opening scene depicts the shepherds and their flocks; the fair being an established institution, it attracts people from miles around. Gabriel attends in his official function. There is a vivid account of the entry of the flocks, with here and there a shepherd 'like a gigantic idol amid a crowd of prostrate devotees' (p. 397). We note almost in passing Hardy's detailed knowledge of the various types of sheep. The attraction of the tent advertising the performance, followed by the crowded atmosphere of pushing and arguing, conveys the authentic excitement of the scene. Hardy briefly recounts Troy's activities in retrospect to explain his sudden appearance here. One of the reasons he has not presented himself again at Weatherbury is his fear that he may have to support Bathsheba. With typical opportunism, he had attached himself to this travelling circus.

Boldwood gets Bathsheba a seat in the tent – she has sold her sheep and has been hoping that Gabriel would appear – and because of the position of her seat she is the centre of attention. Hardy perfectly captures the effect of the light in the tent through a reference to the painter Rembrandt and a description of the sunbeams, which 'spirited like jets of gold-dust' (p. 403). Troy is disconcerted at the sight of Bathsheba and fears her recognition of his voice. At the same time he is again attracted to her – Troy is always susceptible – and ashamed of his position. Troy cunningly suggests that his part should be in mime, so that his voice will not give him away. Poorgrass and Coggan react to the events of the play in a delightfully simple way: the experience will be something to tell their children, says Poorgrass, who touched the hoof of the dead Black Bess.

All the precautions taken by Troy come to nothing when, at the evening performance, he is recognized by the ex-bailiff Pennyways. Later he goes to the refreshment tent and, by placing himself against the canvas of the reserved part, finds that he is virtually embracing Bathsheba, who does not know of his existence. He is greatly drawn to her. Bathsheba's features, as seen by Troy, are described with sexual implication: 'the white shell-like sinuosities of her little ear' (pp. 407–8). A crisis arises when Troy sees Pennyways write a note, since Bathsheba is too proud to listen to what he has to say, to tell her that Troy is there. Troy cleverly extracts the paper from her hand. The narration is as quick and decisive as Troy's action, and the reader's excitement is further roused by Troy's meeting with Pennyways at the end of the chapter.

CHAPTER LI, PP. 410–17

As Joseph is suffering again from his 'multiplying eye', Gabriel is to drive Bathsheba home, but she, as ever given to whims, decides to drive herself, and Boldwood then offers to accompany her on horseback. Bathsheba wishes to be sympathetic to Boldwood in view of her past treatment of him, but this proves to be injudicious, for it revitalizes his 'dream of a Jacob's seven years' service' (p. 411). Bathsheba discourages Boldwood's approaches, telling him how hard it is for a woman 'to define her feelings in language which is chiefly made by men to express theirs' (p. 412). She seeks to deter Boldwood by expressing the fear that Troy still lives – the irony being that indeed he does – but is moved by Boldwood's excited and impassioned attempts to make the bargain with her. His insistence almost forces her to name a time – 'Christmas, we'll say' – when she will give her decision on the promise.

Later Bathsheba confides in Gabriel, telling him that she fears that Boldwood will lose his reason if she does not agree to marry him. Oak is torn in his own advice to her, but his judgement and integrity make him say 'The real sin . . . lies in thinking of ever wedding wi' a man you don't love honest and true' (p. 416). Bathsheba is human enough to feel piqued because in their conversation Gabriel has not declared that he would like to marry her. We feel, though, that her conscience is driving her towards Boldwood.

CHAPTER LII, PP. 418–28

The incongruity of a man like Boldwood's giving a Christmas party is stressed. Bathsheba is rendered doubly sensitive by the fact that she is '*the cause* of the party' (p. 419). There is an immediate contrast between Bathsheba's assertion that she will wear her black silk dress and the elaborate dress preparations of Boldwood. It shows how far apart the two are. We register the quietness of Oak and the fact that Boldwood has a premonition that 'a trouble is looming in the distance' (p. 420). As Bathsheba confided in Gabriel, so too does Boldwood. Boldwood is sensitive to the difference in Oak, observing that he and Gabriel have changed positions. Boldwood's obsession is evident in his exact calculation of the time remaining before he can marry Bathsheba.

This chapter consists of a series of scenes, and in the next we learn that Troy is employing Pennyways as a spy. The ex-bailiff is bitter, but gives a vivid account of the charms of Bathsheba. Troy has already indicated that he finds Bathsheba very attractive again. The lady herself is alternately 'wretched at one time, and buoyant at another' (p. 424). Boldwood, before his world is shattered, generously tells Gabriel that he is going to elevate him in their partnership. Ironically, Boldwood considers he has been successful with Bathsheba through Oak's 'goodness of heart'. The buying of the ring shows Boldwood's fixity of purpose with regard to Bathsheba. Despite the warnings of Pennyways, Troy muffles himself up and decides to present himself at the party. Thus the chapter ends on a note of dramatic expectation.

CHAPTER LIII, PP. 429–39

The gossip of the villagers outside Boldwood's door indicates that Troy has been seen and that he 'means mischief'. The men decide to say nothing to Bathsheba, and it is obvious that they like her greatly, respect her and do not wish to upset her. Boldwood meanwhile waits in great suspense for Bathsheba's arrival. The men see this and feel compassion for him, not realizing until then that he still felt deeply for Bathsheba. They see Troy looking in at the window of the malt-house and listening to the conversation. All talk is of Bathsheba. Laban tries to see her to give her some inkling of the shock that awaits her, but loses his nerve, and later the men go in together.

As Bathsheba prepares to leave, Boldwood comes to her with the question that he must have answered. The air is heavy with their different emotions. She wryly observes of her husband, 'There is considerable doubt of his death' (p. 435), not knowing the terrible manner in which that doubt is shortly to be resolved. Boldwood's impassioned manner leads him to utter the unconsciously prophetic words 'I would give up my life for you!' (p. 435). Bathsheba's promise is wrung from her, and she is further broken down by Boldwood's mastery in forcing the ring upon her.

The change in the atmosphere downstairs is obvious, even, after some moments, to Boldwood. Tall utters the simple but significant words 'O no, sir, nobody is dead' (p. 437), and Troy, announced as a stranger, enters shortly afterwards. The tension is now unbearable. Troy becomes peremptory, while Bathsheba, unable to move at first, indicates her dread by shrinking from him, and then she screams. That scream signals Troy's death, the attempted suicide of Boldwood and his exit into the night in a graphic, dramatic ending to the chapter.

CHAPTER LIV, PP. 440–44

Boldwood immediately gives himself up. Gabriel, always the good shepherd, goes to the house, where he finds chaos in the room; the women are huddled 'like sheep in a storm' (p. 440) and the men do not know what to do. Bathsheba astonishes all by her calmness and practicality. She commandeers Gabriel, who rides off for the surgeon, bemused by what has happened. Bathsheba shows her independence and love by having Troy taken home. She does everything that has to be done for her husband, displaying such courage in her loneliness that the surgeon remarks, 'She must have the nerve of a stoic!' (p. 443). That nerve finally gives way, and, as she watches over her sleeping mistress, Liddy learns that Bathsheba blames herself for the incident.

CHAPTER LV, PP. 445–9

The kind of tension generated by waiting for news is evident here, as the rustics comment on the arrival of the judge and return home, though they are anxious to hear of Boldwood's fate. The disturbed state of Boldwood's mind during the previous months is evident from the collection of dresses and jewellery he has assembled for 'Bathsheba Boldwood'. His sentence comes as no surprise, and it is the following petition that provides the drama of the narrative. It is accentuated when Gabriel sees the scaffold being erected. Bathsheba is not yet fully recovered, and it is obvious that she is becoming increasingly dependent upon Gabriel. The latter is dis-

tressed by the thought of Boldwood dying, 'for there had been
qualities in the farmer which Oak loved' (p. 449). When the news
of the reprieve is made known, Coggan is moved to exclaim, 'God's
above the devil yet!' (p. 449).

CHAPTER LVI, PP. 450–59

Bathsheba gradually revives and in the late summer she begins to go
out. She visits the grave in which she has had Troy buried with
Fanny, an action that marks her developing character, from vain girl
to mature and compassionate woman. The children's singing, and
particularly the words of the hymn, move her to tears. Even after the
arrival of Oak, the words continue to punctuate her consciousness
and emphasize her own past and present. She becomes perhaps more
deeply concerned when she realizes that Gabriel is going to leave her.
She is so distressed that she upsets him. As the weeks pass she notices
that he shuns her company. With the passing of the year to Christmas,
Bathsheba finds it strange that she is brooding not on past events but
on present circumstances, namely Gabriel's defection. His letter final-
izes matters, and Bathsheba, deeply disturbed at the prospect of
losing him, bravely pays him a visit. She learns, after the initial
awkwardness, that Gabriel is concerned about the local gossip, which
suggests that he is hanging about in the hope of marrying Bathsheba.
There is a wonderful play on the words 'absurd' and 'soon' before
Gabriel and Bathsheba come together. Their recognition of their love
is treated with humour. Hardy ends the chapter by philosophizing on
the strength of the kind of love that is complemented by mutuality of
interests.

CHAPTER LVII, PP. 460–65

The decision to have a quiet wedding is natural in view of Bathsheba's
and Gabriel's sensitivity to gossip. Gabriel confides in Coggan, who
warns him that Laban Tall's wife 'will horn it all over parish in half-

an-hour' (p. 461). Coggan's scheme to forestall her works well and Oak joins the conspiracy and contributes to the humour of the situation. There is humour too in the report of the nervous Bathsheba waking Liddy the next morning. The simplicity of the arrangements, the lack of ostentation, the gathering of the rustics in celebration and Oak's accomplished use of 'my wife' all contribute to the final happiness of lives scarred by suffering and ennobled in survival.

Characters

GABRIEL OAK

In the Bible Gabriel is an archangel, the bringer of good news; oak is synonymous with durability and permanence. The hero of this novel lives up to his names in the sense that he represents goodness on the one hand and loyalty on the other. Gabriel is the moral centre of the novel, the pivot around which all else turns. Through him we are given our first sight of Bathsheba, and our first insight into her character comes from his use of the single word 'Vanity' in judgement of her. He is physically tough himself and eccentric in dress, but he has a 'quiet modesty'. His unassuming nature and outward maturity hide a strongly impressionable nature. He demonstrates his capacity for swift decision when he hands the twopence to the gate keeper (p. 55).

Gabriel's history shows that he has made his own way in life, elevated to the title of 'Farmer' through local respect for his 'sustained efforts of industry and chronic good spirits' (p. 59), which made him able to lease the small sheep-farm. He at first seems a solitary man, whose recreation is his flute-playing and whose company consists of the dog George and George's misguided son. He has risked much, but is prepared for the hard work – that is part of his nature – involved in tending sheep. His dedication and softness of heart are evident in his treatment of the new-born lamb. His work is his clock, but he has time to contemplate the beauty of the night, and Hardy invests his contemplation with a poetic consciousness. Occasionally he shows that he has an inquisitive spirit, as when he looks into the shed and sees Bathsheba, her aunt and the cows. Responding to the atmosphere inside, he 'yawned in sympathy' with the women. There is some pathos in his presentation here, for since he cannot fully distinguish Bathsheba, 'he painted her a beauty' out of 'the want of a satisfactory form to fill an increasing void within him' (p. 64). When Gabriel sees her full physicality on the pony and recognizes a certain boldness in her, he blushes from the effect she has on him. He soon becomes aware of her capricious nature and sensitivity. A 'sympathetic man', he considerately looks away, for he knows she is embarrassed that he has seen her antics on the pony.

If he is drawn to her here, his love is more fully confirmed when she saves his life. Hardy likens him to Samson, and certainly this Delilah reduces him quickly. His gratitude and earnestness are immediate, and he holds her hand 'curiously long'. Despite his naturally withdrawn and reticent nature, from now on he waits to see her. The preparations he makes before proposing to her show the sincerity of the man. His present of the lamb to the girl he loves is evidence of his closeness to nature and his warmth. His natural diffidence causes him to retreat after his encounter with the aunt, but when Bathsheba runs after him he simply assumes that she has come to accept him. Again we are aware of the pathos. His direct expression of his feelings – 'I love you far more than common' (p. 78) – is moving because of its open simplicity. His thinking ahead to provide the kind of things he supposes Bathsheba would like, such as a piano, shows his awareness, perhaps too readily admitted, of his inferior status. It also reflects his uncertainty. He is deeply moved when Bathsheba turns him down. His voice has 'a genuine pathos now, and his large brown hands perceptibly trembled' (p. 80). His guileless sincerity of approach has told against him.

Oak suffers adversity, and his character assumes tragic proportions. He is 'an intensely humane man', and the destruction of his flock leads him to feel compassionately for his sheep. Yet his most striking reaction, which shows the genuine unselfishness of the man, is his thankfulness that he is not married, as otherwise his wife (i.e. Bathsheba) would have had to endure 'the poverty now coming upon me' (p. 86). He gains in dignity what he has lost materially, and we note particularly his resilience in misfortune. His attempts to hire himself out as a shepherd seem doomed to failure because of his honesty, for he reveals, when questioned, that he had his own farm. He cheerfully resorts to his flute, however, and is apparently not ashamed to earn a few pence. When he makes for Weatherbury, he broods on his losses in love and in life – he is 'introspective far beyond his neighbours' (p. 91). Governed by Fate like so many of Hardy's characters, he leaves the waggon at a spot from where he can see the fire. He acts decisively and heroically, showing practicality and qualities of leadership, which we might not have suspected in view of his diffidence. He moves from public crisis to private kindness in his meeting with the unknown Fanny Robin. He soon sinks his own humiliation at being called 'Only a shepherd'. He gives the suffering Fanny money and treats her with warmth from the heart.

He quickly commands the respect of his new workmates at Warren's by his modest demeanour. He adjusts himself to this company, reveals a delicious sense of humour – 'I never fuss about dirt in its pure state' (p. 105) – and succeeds easily in becoming accepted. He is intent on finding out what he can about Bathsheba, but the natural garrulity of the company makes this difficult. Instead he adapts himself to the level of conversation, propitiates the maltster, and so employs his flute that he wins himself friends.

When he begins to work for Bathsheba, Gabriel is 'rather staggered by the remarkable coolness of her manner' (p. 131). He quickly finds himself occupied with the lambing, making practical use of the malthouse. He responds warmly to anything that is said about Bathsheba, and such is his continuing interest that he goes so far as to question the men individually about her, thus indicating his inclination and also his protective attitude towards her. After threatening anyone who takes her name in vain, Oak modestly reveals that he would like to be the new bailiff of the farm in place of the thieving Pennyways.

Gabriel gets to know Boldwood through Fanny Robin's letter and by identifying Bathsheba's writing for him. Although Boldwood becomes infatuated with Bathsheba, Oak always treats him with respect and, as the affair develops, with heartfelt compassion. With the fine sensitivity that distinguishes him on all occasions, Gabriel recognizes that Boldwood's sufferings over Bathsheba are much greater than his own. As yet, however, Gabriel only suspects Bathsheba of 'some coquettish procedure'. This is reinforced when he finds that Bathsheba is intent on sounding him out about what the men have observed of herself and Boldwood (Chapter XX). He has the courage and the audacity to reprove her for her conduct, and even to criticize her further. The result is inevitable. Gabriel, 'held to her by a beautiful thread . . . rather than by a chain he could not break' (p. 186) is sacked and leaves the farm immediately.

The crisis of the sick and dying sheep ensures his early return. From that time Gabriel is the man who deals with practical and emotional crises, as far as Bathsheba is concerned. The 'clever man in talents!' tells Bathsheba, via Laban Tall, that *'beggars mustn't be choosers'*, but the reader, knowing of Gabriel's compassion for the suffering of any creature, realizes what it must have cost him to say this. The 'love-led man' returns, after putting his practical skill to the saving of life, to the bondage of being near Bathsheba and the contemplation of her successive errors. The sheep-shearing finds Gabriel the naturally accepted general supervisor. We are constantly made aware of his capacity for practical responsibility. Throughout this particular sequence he shows himself hypersensitive to the proximity of Bathsheba. He becomes 'constrained and sad' as he watches the apparent intimacy of Bathsheba and Boldwood. This causes him to make a rare slip; he snips a sheep in the groin and brings a strong reprimand from Bathsheba. That evening he has to move from his appointed seat at the table to accommodate Boldwood. He finds that his suspicions about Boldwood's bearing towards Bathsheba are confirmed. For Gabriel there is merely the temporary pleasure of accompanying Bathsheba's singing on his flute.

The advent of Troy into Bathsheba's life pushes Gabriel firmly into the background. He has the character – and lack of tact – to approach Bathsheba on the subject of Troy. He provides himself with the excuse that she is treating Boldwood unfairly, interrupts her walk at dusk one evening, and seeks to turn the conversation to Troy by introducing the subject of 'bad characters'. He immediately shows his boldness by referring to the wedding of Bathsheba to Boldwood, which people anticipate is to take place. Unaware of her feelings, he unwisely refers in derogatory fashion to Troy. He follows this with a dignified affirmation of his own love for Bathsheba, and then counsels her to be 'more discreet in your bearing towards this soldier' (p. 248). When she responds by threatening to dismiss him for the second time, he shows a rare spirit of obstinacy in refusing to be ordered away. We know that he is moved by his desire to protect her and by his love for her, but there is a certain nobility and selflessness too in his trying to save the impetuous Bathsheba from her own emotional folly. When he leaves Bathsheba he suspects that she wants to get rid of him because she has arranged to meet Troy, and he proceeds to check up on Troy's story about his secret attendance at church. He finds, as he expected, that Troy has lied. He knows too that he is not mistaken about his man.

When Bathsheba unexpectedly goes to Bath, Gabriel has the ingenuity (not appreciated by his mistress later) to commandeer Boldwood's horses. On finding that it is Bathsheba that he has been chasing, Gabriel, disconcerted but as loyal as ever, binds Coggan to secrecy about the night's events. He is always mindful of Bathsheba's reputation among her men and in the locality. When Cain Ball returns from Bath Gabriel is on tenterhooks to find out more about Bathsheba. Cainy's delays only add to Gabriel's apprehensions, and he is forced to adopt 'a despairing attitude of patience' (p. 279). After Bathsheba returns Gabriel is delusively relieved. He does not know until the next day that Bathsheba has married Troy. His own suffering is acute when he sees Troy in full possession at the marital window. He tries to accept it bravely, even argues with Troy about the nature of the house, but his pride makes him reject Troy's money for a drink. It is typical of Gabriel's nobility of nature that when he saw the obvious anguish of Boldwood he 'rose above his own grief' (p. 296).

Gabriel's responsibility and care are seen to advantage in his watchful protectiveness over Bathsheba. The night of the harvest supper and dance finds him saving the ricks, while Troy and the men lie drunk. His observation of the natural phenomena that signal the storm displays his closeness to the countryside. Gabriel shows a concern for the financial losses that might accrue to Bathsheba, and once convinced of near disaster, he acts swiftly, as Matthew Moon and the lugubrious Mrs Tall would testify. As always his practicality, this time with some help from the unhappy Bathsheba, saves her from misfortune. They share the labour, the crisis of the lightning, and the knowledge of Bathsheba's failing marriage. This experience is one of the bases from which their own love develops. After Bathsheba has left, having confided warmly in Gabriel, he ponders on 'the contradictoriness of that feminine heart' (p. 312). He works on, remembering the fire some eight months previously and thinking of his 'futile love of the same woman', though he is 'generous and true, and dismissed his reflections' (p. 313).

Gabriel never loses his capacity to be astonished. He shows this when he realizes that Boldwood has not bothered to cover up his own ricks. His compassion for the man reflects his own stoicism. *His* responsibilities are never neglected and he is critical of those who are careless about their duties, as when he reprimands Joseph Poorgrass for drinking too much when he should have been bringing the body of Fanny Robin to Weatherbury. He takes over himself, finds that the coffin must be left at Bathsheba's for the night and, in order to spare Bathsheba misery, deletes the words '*and child*' from the chalk scrawl on the coffin-lid (pp. 350–51). Later he unconsciously exercises an effect on Bathsheba as she looks in through the window and sees him praying; she in turn, following his example, prays in her anguish. After Troy's presumed death Gabriel is elevated at last to be Bathsheba's bailiff, taking charge too of Boldwood's Lower Farm. Gabriel becomes the subject of gossip, for he is thought to be 'feathering his nest fast'. Moreover, he is to have a share of Boldwood's profits.

Gabriel again becomes the recipient of Bathsheba's confidences, here with regard to the insistence of Boldwood that she should give him her word – 'the conditional promise' – to marry him. Thus Gabriel unwittingly plays some part in the unfolding tragedy. He is motivated by the best possible reasons, unselfish and noble in origin, namely his compassion and respect for Boldwood and his knowledge that Bathsheba would be truly loved for herself if she married him. Gabriel also feels at this stage that he stands no chance with her. His only reservation is that he knows that Bathsheba herself does not love Boldwood. His coolness amazes Bathsheba, and she is piqued by it. If only Gabriel had declared that *he* would wait for her, she would have been better pleased. Gabriel, for all his love for her, does not comprehend the 'centremost parts of her complicated heart' (p. 417).

Gabriel now considers the change in Boldwood. He gives the latter the impression that he is cynical with regard to love, doubtless because of his past rejection by Bathsheba. Boldwood himself generously refers to Gabriel's 'goodness of heart'. He wishes to make Gabriel his partner, but the latter, with a prophetic instinct, tells him not to think of the future since 'So many upsets may befall 'ee' (p. 425). Truer words were never spoken in apprehension. Although Gabriel is not present in the house to see Troy's return or Boldwood's murder of him, he responds as we should expect to Bathsheba's crisis. As he rides on her errand for the surgeon, he feels that he might have been better employed finding out what has happened to Boldwood. He has, all along, doubted the farmer's sanity. Later, with typical loyalty and compassion, he goes to say goodbye to Boldwood. His sensitivity is such that at this time and afterwards he avoids Bathsheba, thinking of her suffering and of the gossip. The integrity that is the hallmark of Gabriel's character is evident when we are told that his 'anxiety was great that Boldwood might be saved, even though in his conscience he felt that he ought to die' (p. 449).

Owing to the gossip about himself and Bathsheba, Gabriel tries to escape from the situation, and even thinks of leaving England. Their usual conversational naturalness is killed when he gives her the news, and the result is that Gabriel leaves in embarrassment. Bathsheba realizes how much she needs him — she always has — and when she visits him she comes to learn the main reason for his wishing to go. And even here the 'love-led man' has to be led again. Bathsheba makes the running, and Gabriel begins to enjoy the luxury of the love he has so much deserved. Loyalty, self-sacrifice, considerateness, devotion, all those qualities, which have been expressive of his love, ensure their future happiness. So pleased and aware of his new situation is he that, when the men come to congratulate them, he uses the word 'wife' rather readily and puts himself in the way of some mild satire. The course of true love has not run smooth, but Gabriel, with exemplary resilience, has overcome obstacles and suffering through the fullness of his maturity and inherent wisdom.

BATHSHEBA

The Bathsheba of the Bible, the wife of David and the mother of Solomon, was initially wayward like the heroine of *Far from the Madding Crowd.* Hardy's Bathsheba is vain and impetuous, proud but vulnerable. We can see clearly the nature of the girl throughout the action of the story. The word 'girl' is used here because, although there has been much suffering in her life since the sending of the valentine, she is only 'three or four-and-twenty' when she marries Gabriel. Before that, in the aftermath of Troy's death, she takes all decisions and undertakes all immediate actions. As Hardy puts it, 'She was of the stuff of which great men's mothers are made' (p. 441). In the course of the novel the girl who takes out the mirror in Chapter I is transformed into the smiling, but not often laughing bride of Chapter L V I I. What happens to her in between is a triumph for Hardy's art. He shows her character in development, undergoing change, experiencing adversity and passing happiness, emerging stoically into maturity, still vulnerable, still unable to stand alone emotionally, and always human enough to reveal her feelings and her needs. Bathsheba is assured of the reader's sympathy and interest throughout, because although she is often in error, her responses are essentially human and recognizable.

She is sitting on the 'apex' of the waggon when Gabriel first sees her, and we come to appreciate that she is going to have a great fall. She is a girl of unpredictable and impetuous whims: she looks in the mirror and smiles; she drops 'backwards flat upon the pony's back' (p. 65); and, most importantly, she sends the valentine, which has 'MARRY ME' on the seal. Her obstinacy is shown in her refusal to pay the twopence to the turnpike-keeper, her pride in her not deigning to speak to Gabriel, who pays the money and thus loses her her point.

Despite her outward independence, as shown, for example, in her unusual way of sitting on the pony when she thinks no one is looking, Bathsheba has a conventional sense of the class difference between herself and Gabriel and responds to Troy's cosmopolitan and dubiously higher birth. She is self-conscious and aware of her good looks, but embarrassed that Gabriel has seen her riding performance. After she has saved Gabriel, who awakes with his head in her lap, she shows her sense of humour. She is teasing, skittish, and she enjoys a kind of flirtation, but does not over-dramatize what she has done.

She runs after Gabriel, literally and in part metaphorically, impetuously telling him the truth about herself, namely that she has never had a young man. She realizes that she has put herself in an absurd position, but is forthright enough to discourage Gabriel. Even here she gives rein to a kind of winsome humour – she doubts whether she can think outdoors, for 'my mind spreads away so' (p.78). We note that Bathsheba is playing, and the thought of marriage *without* a husband is part of her little fantasy. She also shows a degree of self-knowledge when she says to Gabriel 'I want somebody to tame me . . . and you would never be able to, I know' (p. 80). Here she reads herself and Gabriel correctly, but her pride responds to his honesty with rejection, haughtiness and 'a merry-go-round of skittishness' (p. 82).

Bathsheba's change of fortunes when she is elevated to her own farm finds her adapting to her situation, but still liable to behave in an inconsistent or irrational manner. She is generous, as may be seen in her treatment of her own men, and open. She shows her genuine concern for Fanny Robin, for whom she feels some responsibility, and observes, with unconscious irony in view of what is to occur, 'I do hope she has come to no harm through a man of that kind' (p. 119). She is naturally upset by the dishonesty of the bailiff Pennyways. She confides in Liddy that she has had a proposal, though she does not name Gabriel. The friendship between the two women develops into one of sympathetic love. Bathsheba naturally wishes to assert that she is a woman of experience, and we note the pathos of this. Her attitude to her men is admirably direct, and she easily assumes the reins of authority. Again she shows her sense of humour when she cuts short, though not unkindly, the stammering thanks of Andrew Randle. Her address to the men is indeed impressive: 'I shall be up before you are awake; I shall be afield before you are up; and I shall have breakfasted before you are afield. In short, I shall astonish you all' (p. 133).

The impression is given that Bathsheba rather enjoys her attendance at market. She is thought to be 'headstrong', but one observer considers that 'she'll soon get picked up' (p. 141). Although she is sensitive at being the focus of attention, she is intrigued by the silent and apparently impregnable Boldwood. There follows the sending of the valentine, done in a moment of impetuous thoughtlessness. As Hardy observes, 'Of love as a spectacle Bathsheba had a fair knowledge; but of love subjectively she knew nothing' (p. 148). When she sees Boldwood's eyes on her the following market-day, she becomes aware of her 'misdirected ingenuity', and this spoils the quality of her triumph. She is now in a dilemma; she almost resolves to beg Boldwood's pardon, but cannot do so for fear of offending him.

Although she determines 'never again, by look or by sign, to interrupt the steady flow of this man's life' (p. 174), she is in effect already the prisoner of her own past impulse.

When Boldwood proposes to her at the sheep-washing Bathsheba acts with dignity. As he becomes more passionate she speaks with emotional regret of the valentine as 'a wanton thing which no woman with any self-respect should have done' (p. 179), damning her own thoughtlessness. But all this comes too late. 'Her heart was young, and it swelled with sympathy for the deep-natured man who spoke so simply' (p. 179), which shows her generosity of feeling and spirit. Later she becomes calmer and more dispassionate as she considers the offer; she holds Boldwood in esteem, but does not want him, besides which she still enjoys the nature of her independence as a farmer. Yet she is disquieted – and this reflects the moral core in Bathsheba, which complements the much stronger moral awareness in Gabriel, feeling that as she began it all with the valentine, she 'ought in honesty to accept the consequences' (p. 182). With one of those wonderful transitions that are part of her personality she talks to Gabriel to find out what the men think. She feels some guilt that they have seen her with Boldwood, fearing that they will draw conclusions. Her pride is injured when Gabriel tells her that her conduct is 'unworthy of any thoughtful, and meek, and comely woman' (p. 185). She loses her temper and sacks Gabriel, insulted because he has been honestly outspoken and piqued because he has not said that he loves her. Although Bathsheba's eyes flash in her temper, it is significant that they don't meet Gabriel's. Perhaps that little core of conscience tells her that she is wrong.

Bathsheba has little time for regret, for the next day the sheep are stricken and the presence of Gabriel is essential. The proud woman is forced to bow, but before that she weeps with compassion for the sheep and bitterly at her own humiliation. When Gabriel arrives she looks full of gratitude, though her spoken reproach is at variance with this. However, she smiles 'winningly' when she asks him to stay on.

Her role during the sheep-shearing is a supervisory one and she takes her duties very seriously. After the arrival of Boldwood she speaks to Gabriel with a 'dominative and tantalizing graciousness'. At the supper she is obviously excited, and sings the song that carries such ironic overtones in view of her later meeting with Troy.

Boldwood causes her to lose some of her self-confidence and, unwisely, she agrees to try to love him. She is struggling to atone for what she regards as her sin, but contrives successfully to put off a final answer.

Bathsheba herself now becomes the plaything of Fate, for on that same evening she meets Troy in the fir plantation. She is dazzled by his personality and vulnerable to his sexual proximity. He gives her what she needs – flattery – and Liddy later complements this by telling her of the romance of Troy's birth. Although she is half-angry when she sees Troy in the field, from now on she is compelled by him, finding him irresistible. The 'Queen of the Corn-market' is a vulnerable and inexperienced girl, fascinated in spite of her better moral self and showing her weakness for him in unguarded statements. His facile expression of love and the offer of the watch overcome her. She *wants* to believe everything that he says. The hiving incident brings her again into the orbit of sexual proximity, while the sword-exercise has even more strongly sexual suggestions of manipulation, compulsion, domination and fear. Bathsheba is at the mercy of the fluent and dexterous sergeant. The scene of the sword-exercise represents a kind of symbolic rape, though the climax here is only a parting kiss. Later, when Gabriel taxes her, Hardy uses the image of the trapped robin to describe her imprisonment and anger. As she eagerly tells Gabriel about Troy's going to church through the little door in the tower (p. 247), we know that she is completely infatuated. She now believes everything he says.

In an impetuous reaction to Gabriel's strictures she writes dismissively to Boldwood. She overhears the kitchen gossip about herself and Troy and seeks reassurance from Liddy about him. She feels her own weakness, observing that 'Loving is misery for women always' (p. 254). Her letter to Boldwood having been delivered, she tries in vain to avoid a confrontation with him. She pities him, but tells him that because of her 'unprotected childhood in a cold world' (p. 261) she is not gentle. She is astounded by the 'wells of fevered feeling' in Boldwood, and intuitively – prophetically – fears for Troy's safety. As Hardy puts it, 'this guideless woman too well concealed . . . the warm depths of her strong emotions' (p. 264). Her trip to Bath is misguided. She trusts herself to use strength when she sees Troy, but she only has to see him to be aware of her weakness. Their marriage is inevitable as long as Troy sees advantages to himself arising from it.

It is a constant theme in Hardy's later novels (doubtless from an autobiographical basis), that some marriages carry disillusion and disenchantment with them. Troy asserts his will at the supper and ignores Bathsheba's appeal to him not to give the men strong drink. The result is that she finds herself helping Gabriel to save the ricks. This is accompanied by an awakening consciousness of her husband's true, deceitful nature. She also confesses, in a most poignant admission, that she married Troy because she feared she would lose him. She is tender and soft to her husband in order to get him to change his ways. It is too late, however, and she is overtaken by bitterness when she realizes that Troy no longer has any time for her. She has lost her pride, and hates herself for what she has done. She is plunged deeper into crisis with the death of Fanny, the owner of the golden hair, which she knows Troy treasures. Her talk with Liddy convinces her, rightly, that Troy was Fanny's lover. Nevertheless, she makes generous and seemly preparations for Fanny's burial. When Troy arrives to find Fanny dead, he kisses her, calls her 'my very, very wife!' and tells Bathsheba 'You are nothing to me – nothing' (p. 361).

Bathsheba escapes from the house and spends the night outside, and she becomes more than ever dependent upon Liddy. She determines to make the best of her marriage, 'though this may include the trifling items of insult, beating, and starvation' (p. 366). She does not lose her sense of humour, choosing books that have titles with an ironic bearing on her own situation. When she sees Troy's memorial to Fanny she wipes 'the mud spots from the tomb' (p. 381), almost as if she is cleansing Fanny from sin, and departs with an air of quiet dignity.

Bathsheba is a little relieved that her husband is absent, but she does not initially accept the fact that he is dead. It is as though taken in by him in life, she refuses to let herself be taken in again by this last grotesque happening. Her attractions – and the prospect of money – make her husband want to return to her. On the drive back from the fair she realizes that Boldwood is as impassioned and determined as ever. When he asks for a promise, she prevaricates, registering the febrile excitement of the man as she does so. Eventually she concedes that she will not marry anyone else 'whilst you wish me to be your wife, whatever comes' (p. 414). She confides in Gabriel again – how dependent she is on him – but she cannot remove her responsibility for Boldwood's state from her own conscience. Bathsheba's choice of dress for the Christmas party shows that she wishes to look subdued; she does not want to appear too attractive to Boldwood, for she fears that people may think that she is setting out to captivate him. When Troy enters she is stricken with immobility: 'Bathsheba was beyond the pale of activity – and yet not in a swoon' (p. 438). After his death, as we have noted, she responds with characteristic courage and stoicism, though she calls it 'The heart of a wife merely' (p. 443). It is only afterwards that she faints.

Bathsheba is overtaken by a low fever, and does not recover until the spring. Solitary for some time, she visits the grave of Troy and Fanny in the summer. It is very significant that she has had him buried with her; she recognized the truth of their love and was loyal to them both. She herself is coming back to life, moved by the hymn-singing, just as earlier she had been moved by seeing Gabriel pray. Her dependence on Gabriel, and finally her love for him, overtakes her. It is a tribute to her resilience and her sense of what is right, the moral development in her character, that she should go to him. She has moved from vain innocence through intolerable suffering to quietly joyous love. Bathsheba is a thoroughly convincing character, warm, volatile, wayward, impetuous; she alternates between strength and weakness, but never for a moment places herself outside the reader's sympathy.

FRANCIS TROY

Troy is heard rather than seen in his introduction to the reader when Fanny Robin goes to his barracks. His words reveal the selfishness of the man: his statement 'It was a wonder you found me here' (p. 137) implies that he expected to escape from her, and that she would not have the nerve to follow him. The dialogue centres on Fanny's attempts to arrange their marriage. Troy, being devious and delaying, is adept at half promising but in reality not committing himself. The fact that Fanny is humiliating herself and that she is obviously a decent and modest girl does not seem to bother him. The next time we see him (Chapter XVI), Troy himself is humiliated as he waits for Fanny, who has gone to the wrong church. His treatment of her here is a mixture of 'light irony' and bitterness. Despite having been the focus of attention and gossip, Troy, we feel, is perhaps a little relieved that he has not yet been trapped into marriage.

Troy is essentially an opportunist. When he encounters Bathsheba in the fir plantation, he has only to see her face to begin flirting, flattering, actually touching her hand and then apologizing. He dominates her verbally and physically by his presence. We learn that he lives only for the present, that he lies easily to women and that he has a quick understanding, but no depth or the will-power to follow a set purpose. Ironically, he has one quality in common with Bathsheba — he is impetuous. He is educated, fluent and persuasive. Hardy devotes virtually a whole chapter to describing him (Chapter XXV). Troy's attitude to women, somewhat borne out by his later attitude to Bathsheba, is to flatter and then, if that fails, to curse. Some of his opportunities he makes for himself, certainly with regard to the haymaking and the hiving of the bees. His fluency disconcerts Bathsheba, but from calling her the 'Queen of the Corn-market' to offering her his watch is a small step in the progression of his courtship. He has the instinctive wisdom to tell her that she is beautiful, and she herself notes the winning nature of his talk. With facile naturalness he tells her that he loves her, and when she doubts him and unconsciously reveals her own wish to believe what he says, he becomes serious and temporarily curbs his fluency. He receives back the watch, but says that he himself may be caught.

The sword-exercise is Troy's triumph. His explanations are the prelude to dexterity. His talk of missing is accompanied by the innuendo that he does not miss where it matters: he gets through, so to speak, to her heart in this demonstration. The lock of hair shows his power, and the scene has all the threat and glamour and the suddenness of sexual passion. When he buttons up the lock and then kisses her he is showing just how irresistible he is. Troy paces his courtship perfectly. He knows that by going he is leaving her to the contemplation of his magnetic performance and personality.

Troy is not simply a liar, he almost enjoys deception for its own sake. When he is confronted by Boldwood after he has secretly married Bathsheba, Troy leads Boldwood on to offer him money to marry Fanny. He teases Boldwood rather cruelly as he urges him to listen to what he says to Bathsheba: 'It will help you with your love-making when I am gone' (p. 287). What Boldwood does hear is enough to make him nearly kill Troy, in an anticipation of what occurs later. Troy flippantly suggests that Boldwood should kill himself. He is amazed that the infatuated man now transfers his offer of money to a settlement on Bathsheba if Troy marries her; the terrible irony is that Troy already has. His passing out to Boldwood of the report of the marriage is followed by an overtly sadistic 'low gurgle of derisive laughter' (p. 291). Troy throws back the money in a way that shows how much he enjoys being in command. Behind his action is the knowledge that he now commands Bathsheba and her money.

Troy enjoys his new power. Next morning, in the full flush of his triumph, he condescends to *his* employees by giving them money for a drink, while at 'The Revel' he gets everybody drunk, including himself. He has contradicted Gabriel about the ricks – he is of course proved wrong – and shown himself to be irresponsible on the one hand and dismissive of his wife on the other. Bathsheba explains to Gabriel that she married Troy in order to keep him for herself. In Bath he had told her that he had seen a woman who was more beautiful than she was and he could not promise to be faithful. This is typical of Troy's attitude. The moment rules, he is naturally fickle, careless of hurting, impervious to all but his own selfish whims and needs. Soon he reveals that he is a gambler. He humiliates Bathsheba when she reasons with him – 'turn on the water-works; that's just like you' (p. 318) – and again at the meeting with Fanny Robin on the road. His philosophy is a simple one: 'All romances end at marriage' (p. 330). After the interrogation over the lock of yellow hair, he openly says, 'If you repent of marrying, so do I' (p. 332). If his treatment of Bathsheba here is cruel, that cruelty is compounded by his sadism when he returns home to find Fanny dead. He refers to Fanny as his wife and kisses her in front of the shaken Bathsheba, who has only just learned of Fanny's child and knows that Troy must be the father. He behaves 'heartlessly', telling Bathsheba, 'I am not morally yours' (p. 361). He then indulges his romanticism. The tomb, the grave and the flowers are the symbols of his remorse, but it would be wrong to pretend that the feeling runs deep. When the gurgoyle has finished its destruction, we are told that 'Troy had a power of eluding grief by simply adjourning it'. He has suddenly reached a stage where he 'hated himself' (p. 377), which makes him decide to leave. It is the nearest he comes to an admittance of his true character, for on no other occasion does he ever consider rejecting himself.

His travels and reappearance at the fair may seem improbable, but given Troy's nature and his opportunism, they are not incompatible with what we already know of his behaviour. He nearly panics when he sees Bathsheba, yet he turns things to his advantage by dexterously stealing Pennyways's note. He finds himself sensually appreciating his wife and contemplating too the material prosperity she can give him. He is astute enough to employ Pennyways to investigate his position if he reappears from the dead and is found to be guilty of deception. It is never put to the test. His disguise on the fatal night is representative of his capacity for deception throughout his life. He speaks peremptorily to his wife and seizes her arm. Accustomed as he is to indulging his every need, particularly with regard to women, he is fatally foiled. Despite his sentimentality and natural charm, Troy is a thoroughly selfish man who does what he wants when he wants. The feelings of others never come between him and the gratification of his desires.

WILLIAM BOLDWOOD

Boldwood is a gentleman-farmer of little Weatherbury, about forty years old, handsome but stern, and certainly rich. Before we meet him we know of his concern for Fanny Robin. Women in the area have set their caps at him to no avail. To Bathsheba's annoyance, he even inquires of Teddy Coggan if Bathsheba is 'staid'. He is the one man who takes little account of Bathsheba at the market. 'He was erect in attitude, and quiet in demeanour' (p. 141), and Bathsheba notes that his personality is redolent of dignity. This is broken down, as is his obvious pride, when she sends him the valentine. Apparently he was jilted when he was young, and this is to be his fate again. The words 'MARRY ME' fascinate him, and he fights his 'nervous excitability'. After discovering from Oak's recognition of her handwriting that Bathsheba sent the valentine, he appraises her in the market-place. He grows 'hot down to his hands with an incipient jealousy' (p. 168) when she talks to a young farmer. It is the symptom of the illness to come. Such is his intensity of presence that Bathsheba is aware of him and tries to nerve herself to beg his pardon.

Boldwood's lonely reserve conceals a deeply passionate nature, and he now becomes restless and tortured. He lacks humour and is introspective. Consequently, when he decides to approach Bathsheba, he proposes to her directly without preamble and, such is his passion, without romance. Ruled by his feelings, his declarations become importunate. He turns Bathsheba's sending of the valentine into a manifestation of her 'prophetic instinct'. She is moved by his 'deep-natured' appeals. He is earnest and grateful when she agrees to consider what he has said, and goes into a kind of trance when she has gone. After Bathsheba has written to Boldwood to tell him that she cannot marry him, he comes to see her, and describes his feeling for her as 'A thing strong as death' (p. 257). These are terrible words in view of what is to happen. So reduced is Boldwood that he asks for her pity, and his impassioned entreaties to her show the anguish he is experiencing. He displays too his temper and bitterness, telling her that she is heartless and that she doesn't care. The deep anger breeds thoughts of revenge, and he threatens to horsewhip Troy.

When Bathsheba returns from Bath, Boldwood tries to see her, but is refused entry. He walks slowly homeward and encounters Troy. Such is Boldwood's determination and strength that Troy is almost frightened of him. Boldwood quickly develops his plan of buying off Troy by paying him to marry Fanny Robin. It shows that Boldwood is innocent, naïve in the ways of Troy's world, and Troy is thus able to play with him. When he hears Bathsheba and Troy talking, Boldwood is first moved to try to kill Troy – he nearly strangles him – and then to pay him to marry Bathsheba. We note the instability of his nature in this sudden change, yet we sympathize with it, since his main concern is that Bathsheba should have what she wants, whatever the extent of his own suffering. Humiliated by the report of the marriage, Boldwood vows revenge on Troy. He spends the rest of that fateful night walking alone. As always, we are aware of the solitary suffering of the man.

Boldwood obsessed is Boldwood absorbed. He neglects his ricks and Gabriel notices his altered appearance. Despite his introspection,

Boldwood has the natural compassion to see that Gabriel himself looks 'tired and ill'. Such is Boldwood's pride that he has to tell Gabriel, after confessing his grief, that other people had made too much of his affair with Bathsheba.

With Troy's supposed death, Boldwood experiences a resurgence of hope, and cherishes the moment when he held the fainting Bathsheba in his arms. Yet he lives 'secluded and inactive'. He proposes that Gabriel should run the Lower Farm, and bides his time, caught up in the 'fond madness' of his passion for Bathsheba. He even becomes a little devious and cross-examines Liddy about her mistress's intentions with regard to re-marriage. Such is his conscience, however, that he departs ashamed with himself for having done anything that might be thought underhand. After the incident in the tent at the fair, Boldwood drives Bathsheba back home, and exploits the occasion to wring from her a promise that at Christmas she will confirm her intention to marry him.

On the final fateful occasion Boldwood's preparations are sympathetically witnessed and supported by Gabriel. Boldwood even becomes something of a dandy about his dress, and is dismissive of the time he will have to wait for her, now only 'Five years, nine months, and a few days' (p. 421). Bathsheba gives her solemn promise just after Boldwood has said that he will give up his life for her. He does so when Troy's touch on her arm is too much for his already taut nerves. Although he kills Troy, Boldwood never moves outside the range of our sympathies. And when we read of that store of gifts and preparations for 'Bathsheba Boldwood', we realize that his obsession has run into madness. Yet we remember the little kindnesses – helping to drag the pond for Fanny – and the integrity of the man before terrible delusion was brought upon him by the casual whim of Bathsheba.

FANNY ROBIN

Fanny plays little part in the action of the novel, yet it would not be an exaggeration to say that she exercises a major influence on it. She makes her first appearance when Gabriel meets her after he has put out the fire at Bathsheba's farm and is on his way to Warren's Malthouse. She is described as 'a slim girl, rather thinly clad' (p. 99); she has an attractive voice and, despite her being out late, a modest manner. She makes Gabriel promise that he will not reveal that he has seen her 'at least, not for a day or two' (p. 100). Gabriel senses both her sadness and her excitement. Fanny is no ordinary common girl. The scene outside the barracks reinforces our idea of her modesty and sensitivity. She uses the term 'Your wife', though she is not yet married to Troy; the wish is stronger than the fact. She is humiliated, for Troy's disengaged attitude 'makes me say what ought to be said first by you' (p. 137). Pathos attends Fanny and her situation. She knows that she will be thought a loose woman and she even apologizes to Troy for her seeming forwardness. We note, as Oak did, the febrile excitement that has driven her to undertake this journey and to endure the humiliation.

Her letter to Gabriel shows how well-bred and considerate she is. Again she binds him to secrecy, rather proud of the fact that she can announce the marriage and present herself and her husband, as she thinks, in Weatherbury. The confusion over All Saints' and All Souls' finds her anxious once more. At this stage we do not know that she is pregnant, but we might suspect it. Her suffering deepens when she encounters Troy on the highway. She is poverty-stricken and on her way to the workhouse. She recognizes Troy by his voice and faints from exhaustion and shock. Troy gives her money, but she is obviously oppressed by the fact that he is with his wife. There follows her terrible journey to the Casterbridge Union. She feels that she is going to die and shows enormous strength of will despite her physical exhaustion. She improvises the crutches and then clings to the dog who supports her there, only to be stoned away. The incident is one of the most profoundly moving in the novel, since the dog provides Fanny with the warmth and contact lacking for her in humanity. Fanny bears Troy's child and dies, but she lives beyond the grave. Bathsheba, in spite of Gabriel's erasure, knows of the child and knows too that Troy regards the dead Fanny as his wife. Fanny was born to be the victim of such a one as Troy, and his romantic and sentimental effusions about her after her death cannot compensate for his off-hand, even callous usage of her in life.

LIDDY SMALLBURY

Liddy is far more Bathsheba's companion and confidante than a servant. She is the maltster's great-granddaughter, about the same age as Bathsheba; she is not a beauty, but she has a fine complexion. We are told that 'Though elastic in nature she was less daring than Bathsheba, and occasionally showed some earnestness, which consisted half of genuine feeling, and half of mannerliness superadded by way of duty' (p. 122). She asks Bathsheba if anyone has ever wanted to marry her, for she delights in confidences. There is a comic moment when, after Bathsheba has finished paying and addressing the men, Liddy makes her exit in imitation of Bathsheba's dignity. Liddy provides Bathsheba with local information, notably about Boldwood and his sad affair in the past. She also tells the men about the purchases Bathsheba has made, among them a piano.

Since Bathsheba confides in her, wishes to have her opinion (for example, with regard to Troy), and tests her reactions, Liddy becomes very important to her. The dialogue between them before the valentine is sent is important, for Liddy almost acts as devil's advocate for Boldwood by stressing his indifference to womankind and to Bathsheba. After her encounter with Troy in the fir plantation, Bathsheba questions Liddy about Troy, and hears of the glamour and romance attached to him, suitably embellished: 'Such a clever young dand ... He's a doctor's son by name ... and he's an earl's son by nature!' (p. 217). Once in verbal flow, Liddy is capable of running to flood, but there is no doubting the goodness of her heart. Bathsheba has need of her, particularly after she has written the dismissive letter to Boldwood. At first Liddy responds to Bathsheba's assertion that she doesn't care for Troy with supportive statements affirming his fickle nature. But her warmth and sympathy soon discover the truth, and Bathsheba embraces her in her own need for understanding and help. Liddy however, even to comfort her mistress, cannot unsay what she has said or what is said by others about Troy. She is overcome by the force of Bathsheba's passion, and asks to leave: '"I don't see that I deserve to be put upon and stormed at for nothing!" concluded the small woman, bigly' (p. 254). She soon makes it up, however, for she is obviously fond of Bathsheba and moved by her plight.

When Liddy comes back from her holiday, she has to put Boldwood off when he comes to call on Bathsheba, for the latter has secretly married Troy. During the crisis of Fanny's death Liddy answers Bathsheba's queries about Fanny's young man and the colour of her hair. Her talk causes Bathsheba to speak with 'nervous petulance', for she has provided Bathsheba with unconscious confirmation that Troy was Fanny's lover. Bathsheba later asks her if she has heard anything strange about Fanny, but gossip about the child has apparently not reached Liddy. When it does, Liddy immediately tells Bathsheba, diplomatically affecting not to believe it. The next morning Liddy is of positive comfort to Bathsheba, for she searches for her, finds her outside and crosses the swamp to reach her. Though the warm-hearted girl does not understand everything, she speaks to Bathsheba 'with tears in her eyes' (p. 365).

After Troy's death, when Boldwood asks her questions about her mistress's intention over marriage, Liddy shows a sly sense of humour, asking him if he has asked the lawyers whether Bathsheba could remarry or not. On the fateful evening when Troy returns and Boldwood kills him, Liddy comforts her mistress in her agitation. She tries to get Bathsheba to brighten herself up. After that she does not appear in the action until Bathsheba confides in her that she is going to marry Gabriel. Then, and it is typical of her warm nature, she confesses that the news makes her heart go 'bumpity-bump'.

THE RUSTICS

The rustic group in a Hardy novel often performs in a way similar to that of the Greek chorus in a tragedy. The chorus acts as a messenger, it brings news, it comments on the actions of the central characters; sometimes it interprets their actions and sometimes it provides light relief. In Hardy's novels the rustics provide comedy and carry out many or all of the functions mentioned above, but – and this is the major mark of difference – they are strongly individualized. Collectively the group provides too a sense of traditional, agricultural continuity against the impermanence of human relationships. The villagers provide gossip, social particularity and, sometimes, judgement. When Gabriel falls asleep on the waggon going to Weatherbury, for example, he wakes to hear talk that turns out to be about Bathsheba. The group manages to spend much of its leisure time at Warren's Malthouse. The fact that the maltster knows Gabriel's grandfather establishes a kind of rough intimacy and acceptance, and thus performs the function of integrating Gabriel into the neighbourhood. The interaction within the group is comic, particularly on the subject of dirt. There is Mark Clark, with whom everyone drinks and for whom everyone pays. There are Jan Coggan, head-godfather and popular best man, and the self-conscious Joseph Poorgrass, somewhat simple, for whom the world is too much, and whose nervousness and modesty provide a baiting point for some of the others. Jan Coggan contributes plentiful information about Bathsheba's family, and relevant anecdotes too (such as the story of her father lighting the candle three times every night just to look at her mother). There are Susan Tall's henpecked husband, Laban, Henery Fray frightening Joseph Poorgrass with his news, and the bailiff Pennyways, who makes off with Bathsheba's barley.

The first function, then, is to give Gabriel information about Bathsheba and to establish the particularity of local tradition. That done, it is noticeable that the group or one or more of its members is present at the various crisis points of the narrative. An insight into the rustics and their characters is provided in Chapter X, when Bathsheba pays the men and questions them about their work. There is a fine exchange with the stuttering Andrew Randle; we observe the dominance that the 'lawful wife' of Laban Tall exerts, and we note too the names of the field-women Temperance and Soberness. Henery's comment on them is that they are 'Yielding women – as scarlet a pair as ever was' (p. 129). It is William Smallbury who brings the news that Fanny has run away. Henery, Joseph Poorgrass and Mark Clark debate the headstrong nature of Bathsheba and her failure to replace the dishonest bailiff. The lambing leads to more discussion, to which Gabriel closely attends because he will not have anything said against Bathsheba.

The first crisis point is the poisoning of the sheep. Here the rustics, in chorus, tell Bathsheba the news and, effectively persuade her to sink her pride and get Gabriel to come back quickly, since he is the only person who can save her flock. It is noticeable that they themselves form into a flock and follow Gabriel because 'he's a clever man in talents' (p. 189). The sheep-shearing is punctuated throughout with humour, from Henery Fray's ambitions to the veteran pronouncements of the maltster and the wish of Maryann for a mate. The shearing-supper finds them all active; Jan Coggan and Joseph Poorgrass sing; Bob Coggan is sent home for behaving badly, while Pennyways reappears and behaves honestly, according to his ex-mates. When Troy comes to the field at the haymaking, just as when Boldwood appeared and sought her company, Bathsheba is aware of the rustics and their acute observation of what is going on.

Jan Coggan is in some ways the brightest and best of the group, and Gabriel takes him to Bath with him in pursuit, as it turns out, of Bathsheba. Coggan keeps the secret of the night to himself. Much later, Gabriel confides in him alone that he is going to marry Bathsheba.

Bathsheba's absence in Bath provokes a great deal of rustic comment. Cainy Ball's obsession with the place he has visited and his tantalizing narrative provide speculation about Bathsheba's courtship, much to the disquiet of Gabriel. The simple country boy's delight in all the things he saw in Bath endears him to the reader. At the celebration dance and supper the rustics are in good form, but Troy plies them with drink and they are soon overcome. Matthew Moon tells Gabriel mechanically where his tools are, and Mrs Tall, somewhat put out, reveals the whereabouts of the key to the granary. The next crisis point is the death of Fanny, with Joseph Poorgrass acting as messenger and bringing the tidings of the death to Bathsheba. Joseph is deputed to bring Fanny back to Weatherbury, but the oppressive nature of his task and the atmosphere of the fog causes him to break his journey at the inn, where Mark Clark and Coggan encourage him to stay and drink. This results in rustic philosophizing about the death of Fanny and complete inaction, which in turn leads to Gabriel taking over the carriage with the coffin.

With the supposed death of Troy, comment among the rustics embraces Gabriel, who provides a focus of speculation because, as Susan Tall observes, he 'is coming it quite the dand' (p. 391). The sheep fair marks the resurgence not only of Troy, but also of

Pennyways, who hands the note to Bathsheba. Pennyways, still bitter at his treatment by Bathsheba, goes on to become the ally of Troy and makes inquiries for Troy about his legal position. Jan Coggan and Joseph Poorgrass are involved in some scuffling in the tent, and both respond enthusiastically, if naïvely, to the Turpin spectacular.

In Chapter L I I I the rustic chorus assembles on the fateful evening of the Christmas party and of Troy's return. It is this that concerns them. They know what the main characters do not know, and their comments range from fact to sympathy and to rejection: 'He was seen in Casterbridge this afternoon . . . He'll drag her to the dogs . . . one is more minded to say it serves her right than pity her' (p. 429). Their debate centres on whether or not to tell Bathsheba. They overhear Boldwood's expression of passion, some being amazed at what they hear. Laban is deputed to tell Bathsheba, but loses his nerve. Even Boldwood notices the peculiar looks of the men. Just as they are about to say something to Bathsheba, a tap at the door indicates that Bathsheba is wanted. Troy has arrived and, within a minute or so, is dead. The rustic chorus here is part of the conspiracy of Fate. One word might have changed things, just as Pennyways's note to Bathsheba would have done, if it had been read. The rustics are always present, either in the foreground or as a background to the main characters. It is fitting that at the close of the action, after the marriage of Gabriel and Bathsheba, 'Those bright boys, Mark Clark and Jan' (p. 464) and the others should be present. Inevitably they adjourn to Warren's to chew the cud of present news and past history.

Commentary

THEMES

A number of themes run through *Far from the Madding Crowd*, and these will be briefly examined here. Perhaps the major theme is that of loyalty. This is shown in Gabriel's devotion to Bathsheba, which swerves from her for twenty-four hours only, when his outspoken honesty proves too much for her pride, and she dismisses him; it is quickly renewed when he saves her flock from poisoning. His fidelity is Bathsheba's to command, as on the night when he saves the ricks from the storm while Troy and all the men are drunk. Admittedly Bathsheba joins him in this, but his initial motivation arises from his independence and the accuracy of his judgement. Gabriel's loyalty is based on integrity and goodness of heart. It is seen in the concern he comes to show on Boldwood's account; he knows and respects him and fears that he will be disappointed in his love for Bathsheba. Once Oak is loyal, he is always loyal. On the fateful night of the shooting, Oak plays down Boldwood's generosity to him. His later attempt to get away from Bathsheba stems not from disloyalty but from his sensitivity. He recognizes that local gossip has linked their names, and at this stage he has no inkling that Bathsheba has any feelings of love for him. It again reflects his integrity and his capacity for good judgement. Once he knows the state of Bathsheba's heart, he is able to reap the fruits of his selfless devotion to her.

Fanny is as loyal to Troy as he, in what Hardy appropriately calls his romanticism, is to her; the irony is that it is all too late. He is, of course, disloyal to Bathsheba even before Fanny's death occurs. On another important level we note the loyalty of Liddy to Bathsheba, Jan Coggan's to Oak and to his mistress (which is seen in his silence about the events of the night when Bathsheba goes to Bath), and the natural loyalty of the men to Bathsheba (Pennyways is the exception). There is also the tragically misguided constancy of Boldwood to Bathsheba in the obsessive grip of his passionate love.

The theme of love complements that of loyalty at every turn, and the nature of love is variously examined and presented by Hardy. Gabriel's love, as we have seen, is unswerving, as he accepts and tolerates Bathsheba's whims. He endures the vagaries of her disposition, but such is his nature that he is able to put *her* possible happiness (i.e. with Boldwood) before his own. This noble love has a selfless basis, while Boldwood's love, which is an obsession to the point of madness, is the extreme expression of passion. Bathsheba is the first to recognize that she has raised this kind of love through her valentine. Boldwood is capable of taking her impetuosity seriously only because he believes himself loved by her owing to her injunction 'MARRY ME'. Like Gabriel's love, Boldwood's is unchanging, but it is irrational, based on fervour and the movement of his anxious mind. The arrival of Troy and Boldwood's absence at that time thwart him, and Bathsheba's recognition and repentance are too late. Yet Boldwood's love has some unselfish qualities too. He changes from trying to bribe Troy to marry Fanny Robin to urging Troy to marry Bathsheba, once he has overheard how besotted she is with the gallant sergeant. Boldwood's obsessional love is best (or worst) shown in his killing of Troy, as the latter moves to touch Bathsheba, and in his collection of clothes and jewellery labelled with the forward date and the name of Bathsheba Boldwood. Fanny's love for Troy is a long-suffering one, and it ends in her own death. The pathos that is present when she meets Gabriel never leaves her, while the other meetings – outside the barracks and on the highway – show Fanny's love first in humiliating and then in hopeless and degraded circumstances.

Bathsheba's love transforms her life, but only briefly does she achieve happiness. Her love quickly becomes a bitter and an unwarranted experience. It often happens in a Hardy novel that love changes once it has the imprint of marriage stamped upon it. Troy's superficial expression of love for Bathsheba cannot compare with her deep love for him, which precipitates the marriage because she fears that he will turn to another woman. She is possessive in her love, like Boldwood, but she stoically faces the reality of Troy's feeling for

Fanny. She is ennobled by suffering, and has the sense to recognize that her love has been misplaced. The first hint of this is shown on the night of the storm (Chapter XXXVII), which has the significant, prophetic title 'The Two Together'. There are still earlier hints of Bathsheba's dependence on Gabriel in work and crisis on the farm. Her love for Gabriel is carefully defined by Hardy. It develops perhaps as a result of these experiences and has the underlying permanence lacking in romantic infatuation (pp. 458–9):

> This good-fellowship – *camaraderie* – usually occurring through similarity of pursuits, is unfortunately seldom superadded to love between the sexes, because men and women associate, not in their labours, but in their pleasures merely. Where, however, happy circumstance permits its development, the compounded feeling proves itself to be the only love which is strong as death.

Troy's 'love' is obviously lacking in depth. After Fanny's death he rather enjoys tormenting Bathsheba beside the coffin, but he shows little capacity to love her in life. His display of 'love' at the grave is really a compound of repentance and guilt.

In *Far from the Madding Crowd* we are aware of the importance of Fate or destiny in the lives of the characters, and its manifestation sometimes takes the form of coincidence, either casual or at an elevated level. It is casual, for example, when Gabriel goes to Weatherbury on the back of the waggon and happens to jump off at a spot from where he can see the fire, save Bathsheba's property and then work for her. Here we feel that it is destined that he should be near her, while some situations seem to have been contrived by Hardy because they are necessary to his plot, as in the meeting of Troy and Fanny on the turnpike road between Casterbridge and Weatherbury. The elevated, tragic force of coincidence is seen in Troy's first encounter with Bathsheba in the fir plantation, which comes fast on the heels of Boldwood's declaration on the evening of the shearing supper. This meeting changes the course of Bathsheba's life, just as her fateful sending of the valentine had changed Boldwood's (and her own). The chance arrival of Troy in Weatherbury in his circus role of Dick Turpin again initiates a new direction in the action. Linked to the incidence of Fate is the contrivance of man himself. Thus Troy, by presenting himself at the Christmas celebration at Boldwood's, brings about his own fate – death. Similarly Bathsheba, by going to

Bath to renounce Troy, ensures that she will marry him, though this is not her intention. Gabriel, by staying always within reach of Bathsheba, secures the happiness that will ultimately be his. Hardy makes graphic use of Fate — reports that Troy has drowned are generally accepted, but he relates it to the actions of his characters within a given situation.

Most of the humour in the novel is provided by the rustic group in their interactions, their speech and in their individual personalities. Hardy has a fine ear for dialogue and, more particularly, dialogue in dialect. He also has a sharp eye for situation. Frequently, Hardy's humour partakes of pathos as well, and the pathos and the comedy are sometimes interwoven. Thus the shy Joseph Poorgrass adjusts to his blushing inarticulateness, his defect 'filling him with a mild complacency now that it was regarded as an interesting study' (p. 107). He is transformed into 'a man of brazen courage all of a sudden' (p. 108). Jan Coggan misreports him, and he speaks with all the unconscious humour of a wronged man. Mark Clark 'secreted mirth on all occasions for special discharge at popular parties' (p. 106). A number of incidents or scenes are funny: almost the whole of Chapter VIII, entitled 'The Malthouse – The Chat – News', in which Gabriel is integrated into the community, is made up of comic exchanges, innuendoes or situations. Hardy's own delightful humour is evident in the description of his characters, for example where 'a young man about sixty-five' (p. 103) proves to have a son 'Billy, a child of forty' (p. 104). Gabriel's response to being offered 'a clane cup' demonstrates that he is 'a nice unparticular man', further evidenced by his eating the gritty bacon. There is comic anecdote, as when Jan Coggan relates the story of the Everdene parents and the husband's humorous attitude towards his marriage: as long as he thought that he was sinning with his wife 'a got to like her as well as ever, and they lived on a perfect picture of mutel love' (p. 111). Here the humour has serious overtones, the anecdote anticipating in part at least the attitude of Troy towards his marriage to Bathsheba. Some of the humour derives from the rustics' contemplation of their employer, Bathsheba. Her headstrong nature and the quality of her furnishings lead the men to indulge in what Gabriel sternly rebukes as 'dalliance-talk'. Bathsheba's paying of the men, their individual responses and, in some cases, their simple self-consciousness and eccentricity, provides both verbal and situation comedy. When the sheep are poisoned, the men's appraisal of the situation is rather comic, particularly as they edge Bathsheba towards the reappointment of Gabriel for her own good. Another fine humorous sequence, overlaid with Gabriel's tension, occurs as Cainy Ball tells what he saw and did in Bath.

There is a kind of black, almost grotesque comedy in Troy's reappearance in Weatherbury and in his touching Bathsheba through the tent. It also extends to his initial disappearance and presumed death, and earlier to the bringing home of Fanny and her child in the coffin when Joseph Poorgrass delays her return by stopping to drink. The humour often lies in Hardy's contemplation and presentation of his creatures, which is without condescension. The exact ear for simplicity and wit in dialect complements the analysis of character in action and interaction, which is the major focus of Hardy's art.

Irony is, generally, the incongruity of what is expected to be and what actually is. It is obviously present in the situations brought about by coincidence and Fate we have already examined. Irony plays over the presence of Fanny Robin outside the barracks, where she expects, and we might expect for her, the fond return of love for which she has made the journey and perhaps lost her reputation. It is ironic that she has a child, whose existence initially is unknown to both Troy and Bathsheba. Linked to Hardy's use of irony is his use of symbol – something that represents or stands for something else by association. It is possible to see the storm, in which Gabriel saves the ricks and he and Bathsheba come together, as symbolic. Its fury represents the turmoil within Bathsheba regarding the nature of her marriage, and it directly forecasts the future desperate state of affairs between herself and Troy. The lightning flash illuminates for Bathsheba her own situation and her relationship to Gabriel, and at the same time it shows both of them the danger of her present course. Perhaps the gurgoyle is the most obvious of the symbols. A representation of Fate overseeing what Troy has done, its gushings and its destruction and scattering of the flowers that Troy had planted around Fanny's grave indicate his guilt. Hardy's use of symbol is frequently part of his ironic contemplation of the human lot.

OTHER ASPECTS OF HARDY'S ART

Some elements of Hardy's style already mentioned perhaps need particular stress. Dialect – a major ingredient of the humour – and dialogue are both important. The latter is the index to character – as with Boldwood's impassioned 'I want you – I want you to let me say I love you again and again!' (p. 178), or Gabriel's finally delighted 'I've danced at your skittish heels, my beautiful Bathsheba, for many a long mile, and many a long day' (p. 458) – and speech accurately rendered conveys mood. The significant action of the sending of the valentine is instigated by the 'irresponsible Liddy' observing to Bathsheba, 'What fun it would be to send it to the stupid old Boldwood, and how he would wonder!' (p. 146). The lightness of this remark is an ironic comment on the heaviness of the tragedy to come. Hardy's characters speak naturally and effectively within their social register and within their own dramas.

Hardy's narrative is often informed with broad and particular details of his own culture and learning; the Glossary conveys many of his main interests. Analogies drawn from the Bible figure prominently, thus showing the part it played in the lives of simple folk. Hardy also uses classical analogies, for instance referring to Juno, Melpomene and Acheron. There is a wide range of literary reference, which gives the narrative an authoritative stamp and reflects the nature of Hardy's wisdom about life; Shakespeare, Keats, Shelley, Browning are among those quoted or named. The effect is to enhance the reader's appreciation of the story by association. All this is complemented by Hardy's description of nature set, as it so often is, against the vast cosmic perspective of constellations, indicating the smallness of man despite the intensity of his dramas. Norcombe Hill represents part of Gabriel's acquired status, which suffers eclipse with the loss of his sheep. The fir plantation becomes Troy's small empire with the conquest of Bathsheba. Hardy is always intent on natural detail. When first seen by Gabriel, Bathsheba is surrounded by flowers – 'The myrtles, geraniums, and cactuses packed around her were fresh and green' (p. 54), while the decorations planted on Fanny's grave by Troy are as transient as her young life. They are lavished by his too-late love, expressive of his romanticism.

Hardy's love of nature runs throughout his novels, and it is re-flected particularly in his use of metaphor and simile. It inspires some of his richest writing and is a direct indication of the fertility of his imagination. Thus, the maltster, who is very old, is described with 'his frosty white hair and beard overgrowing his gnarled figure like the grey moss and lichen upon the leafless apple-tree' (p. 102). This is at once vivid and imaginative. Hardy's natural imagery is always appropriate: he refers to 'a tongue of air' sucking and drawing the leaves; he describes Bathsheba's positions and flexibility on the horse as being 'like a bowed sapling'; a January day is said to have 'a summer face and a winter constitution' (p. 74); Bathsheba runs after Gabriel 'panting like a robin', her face 'like a peony petal before the sun dries off the dew' (p. 77); when he is rejected, Gabriel heaves a sigh 'like the sigh of a pine plantation' (p. 80); and inside the barn after the harvest supper, drips from an overturned water-jug go down 'the neck of the unconscious Mark Clark . . . like the dripping of a stalactite in a cave' (p. 302).

Not all of Hardy's images are drawn from nature, however. Some-times he makes vivid associations, both pictorially and emotionally, with other subjects, such as when he likens George's son after the destruction of the sheep to 'Napoleon at St Helena'. A series of superb images establishes the atmosphere on the night of the storm (Chapter XXXVII). The lightning 'gleamed in the heavens like a mailed army', while each 'hedge, bush, and tree was distinct as in a line engraving', and a poplar appears 'like an ink stroke on burnished tin' (p. 306). Perhaps the most moving of all the images is the one used when Bathsheba asks Troy if he knows the dead Fanny in the coffin: 'in a small enclosed echo, as from the interior of a cell' (p. 359).

Hardy has a superb sense of place and an awareness of the current agricultural and small-community traditions, which he knew so well as a boy and continued to observe as a man. Such events as the sheep-shearing, the supper that follows it, the annual Weatherbury fair, the dipping of the sheep, the hiving of the bees and the weekly bargaining in the market all give Hardy's work the particularity and permanence of place. On the night of the storm Gabriel notes all the signs, inside and outside, that betoken what is to come. The large toad, 'soft, leathery, and distended, like a boxing-glove' (p. 300), which Gabriel accidentally kicks, has its equivalent inside the house in the 'thin glistening streak' indicative of the garden-slug 'which had come indoors to-night for reasons of its own' (p. 300). *Far from the Madding Crowd* is steeped in agricultural traditions and associations — witness Gabriel at the statute fair and the various occupations of Bathsheba's men and field-women, all with their closeness to the soil. In the seasonal adjustments from the lambing through to a Christmas party like Boldwood's there are crisis points, such as Gabriel's saving of the ricks and Boldwood's forgetting to do anything about his. They are the words and the punctuation of rural life. Gabriel's flute playing, together with the singing and dancing that accompany the small gatherings and larger festivals, typify the leisure activities (with talk and drink) of the community. It is this community that provides the foreground and background of the novel.

Throughout the narrative, while we may be aware of Hardy's pessimism about human relationships (despite the love and re-conciliation of the ending), we sense his overriding love of tradition in the incidents and practices of daily life, which are so meticulously and sympathetically described. There is a love of locality, an appraisal of superstition and a power of seasonal identification and observation, which is traced with a loving hand. Editions of this and other Wessex novels stress the importance of all these elements by providing a map and key to place names (see Penguin edition pp. 37–42). This is in itself a tribute to the feeling and historical actuality with which the novels are imbued and which constitute a major part of their appeal.

Glossary

Abraded: rubbed by the effects of time

Acheron: river of hell in Greek mythology

Adumbrating: outlining, foreshadowing

All a sheenen . . . handlen: quotation from 'Woak Hill', a poem by Hardy's Dorset neighbour William Barnes, whose poetic works Hardy edited

All Saints' and All Souls': title of the chapter that Hardy added to the novel at proof stage. It was not in the manuscript

All-Fours: a card game

Alonzo the Brave: 'Alonzo the Brave and the Fair Imogine', a poem written by M. G. Lewis, tells of the appearance of Alonzo's ghost

Amazonian: acting like an Amazon, a female warrior of classical legend

Antiphonies: sung responses

Aphrodite: in Greek mythology, the goddess of love, daughter of Zeus

Ararat: resting place of Noah's Ark after the Flood, as described in Genesis

Arcadian: in classical legend Arcadia was a region inhabited by shepherds, musicians and the god Pan, who invented and played a seven-reed pipe

As though a rose . . . again: quotation from 'The Eve of St Agnes' (1819) by John Keats

Ash's Dictionary: The New and Complete Dictionary of the English Language (1775)

Ashtoreth: fertility goddess worshipped in Canaan

Attar: oil from flowers used as the basis for perfume

Aurora militaris: warlike brightness

Ayless: always

Ba'dy: low, bawdy

Baking trendle: tray for mixing dough

Balboa: Vasco Muñez de Balboa (1475–1517), Spanish explorer, who was the first European to look out on to the Pacific

Ballet: ballad

Banks of Allan Water: a traditional air

Bathsheba: wife of Uriah the Hittite. She married David after he had killed Uriah; Solomon was her son

Batty-cake: small cake

Better wed . . . moor: proverbial expression meaning that it is better to marry someone who lives nearby rather than a stranger. Mixen is a dunghill

Biffins: Norfolk cooking apples

Board of Guardians: committee responsible for administering the workhouse

Bobbin: round piece of wood tied to the latch-string

Brandise: iron stand on three legs, which holds cooking utensils on the fire

Burning for burning . . . strife: see Exodus xxi: 25

Cabala: secret

Cedit amor rebus: from the Roman poet Ovid's *Remedia Amoris*

Chain Salpae: groups of marine animals, which remain connected to each other

Chamfers: channels, gutters in a column

Chargeable to the parish: assisted by poor relief

Charity-boys: orphans educated at special schools

Cheese-wring: cheese-press separating curds from whey in cheese-making

Chinchilla: grey, named after a South American rodent that has grey fur

Chromis: shepherd in the Roman poet Virgil's sixth Eclogue

Classic Renaissance: period from the mid sixteenth to the early seventeenth century

Club-walking: the regular parish walk at Whitsun

Colloquist: the person who was speaking to him

Combination-service: a service in the Book of Common Prayer, which utters threats and curses against sinners; it is now rarely read

Come-by-chance children: illegitimate

Concurritur – Horrae Memento: 'Battle is joined – in a moment of time', from the first ode in Horace's *Satires*

Contretemps: argument, disagreement

Coped: protected by stone

Corinthian: a dissipated man-about-town of the Regency period

Crimped up: screwed up

Crowner's: coroner's

Cuts: hits with the front of the sword

Cyclops' eye: Cyclops were one-eyed giants, described by Homer

Dame Durden: popular folk-song about a woman who employed five male and five female servants

Danby: probably James Danby (1816–75), English landscape painter noted for vivid colouring

Daniel in her kingdom: in Daniel vi:10 Daniel's determination to pray causes him to be cast into a den of lions

DD: the D below middle D

Death's head: skull as an emblem of mortality

Decalogue: the Ten Commandments

Demesnes: land surrounding a house or manor, retained by the owner for his own use

Desdemona: heroine killed by her husband Othello in Shakespeare's play of the same name

Desk: portable rest with writing materials

Devil's head in a cowl: as if the Devil should be a Christian, i.e. hiding his true nature

Dew-bit: food taken in the field before work began

Diana: virginal Roman goddess of the hunt and the moon

Dibble: tool with a point, which makes holes for seeds

Dick Turpin: the most famous of all highwaymen, he was hanged at York in 1739. He rode from London to York on his mare Black Bess, a feat often celebrated in story, verse and dramatic form

Dr Syntax: William Combe wrote the verses for the celebrated Rowlandson illustrations for the travelling clergyman, a grotesque called Dr Syntax

Dr Johnson: English man of letters and compiler of the first comprehensive English dictionary (published 1755)

Draw-latching: dawdling, walking slowly

Dryads: woodland nymphs in classical mythology

Early Flourballs: type of potato

Elymas-the-Sorcerer: the false prophet who was stricken blind and had to grope about (Acts xiii: 6–12)

En papillion: in swimming, the butterfly stroke

Eros: god of love

Esther: beautiful Jewess, who married King Ahasuerus of Persia

Eve of St Thomas's: 21 December, the shortest day

Fearful joy: quotation from Thomas Gray's 'Ode on a Distant Prospect of Eton College' (1747)

Felon: whitlow, an inflammation of the finger or toe, usually near the nail

Fidgets: trivial matters

Figure of eight heads: Greek conception that a perfectly proportioned body should be eight times the length of its own head

Finials: ornaments on gables

First dead . . . yode: quotation from Sir Walter Scott's poem *Marmion* (published 1808)

First floating weed to Columbus: reference to the fact that when Columbus saw seaweed he knew he was near the shore of the New World

Flaxman: John Flaxman (1775–1826), English sculptor and draughtsman, who drew illustrations to Homer's epic poem the *Odyssey*

Flying: crumbling

Foisted: substitute

Fort meeting Feeble: the strong part of the sword meeting the middle part of the blade or that towards the point

Full of sound . . . nothing: quotation from Macbeth's famous soliloquy after the death of Lady Macbeth (*Macbeth*, V,v)

Gawkhammer: stupid

Genius loci: the spirit of the place

Gerard Douw: Dutch painter (1613–75), who studied under Rembrandt

Gilpin's rig: rig, frolic. It is a reference to William Cowper's celebrated ballad *John Gilpin* (1782)

Gimp: cotton twist with cord or wire in it, used in the trimming of dresses

Gird: mock

Gonzalo: the loyal old courtier in Shakespeare's *The Tempest*

Great Mother: the Roman goddess Cybele

Guards: defensive positions

Guildenstern: courtier employed with Rosencrantz to fool Hamlet (*Hamlet*, II,ii)

Gutta serena: blindness without any difference in the appearance of the eye

Gwine: going

Hapeth: halfpennyworth, a very small amount

Harry: worry

Heart: friend (an exclamation)

Het or wet: rain or shine

Higgling: bargaining

Hinnom: see II Kings xxiii: 10

Hippocrates: Greek physician, who is regarded as the father of medicine

Hiring fair: annual fair, held on 14 February, at which farm labourers offered themselves for employment throughout Britain

Ho and hanker: pine and want

Hobbed: having hobnails

Hobbema: Meindert Hobbema (1638–1709), Dutch landscape painter

Honeycomb-work: patterned like a honeycomb

Horn: spread

Horned man: Devil

Horning: trumpeting

Hylas: in classical legend Hylas, a beautiful youth, was carried off by Hercules with the Argonauts, and was lured away by nymphs and drowned

Hyperbolic curve: curve made when a cone is intersected by a plane

Incarnadined: coloured, given some complexion

Indurating: making hard

Injured Lover's hell: quotation from Milton's *Paradise Lost* (published 1667)

Ixion: According to the Greek legend, Ixion, who had tried to seduce Hera, the wife of Zeus, was punished by being chained to a perpetually revolving wheel of fire

Jacquet Droz: Pierre Jacquet-Droz (1721–90), Swiss clockmaker, who designed celebrated clockwork figures

Javelin-men: the retinue of a sheriff, which bore pikes and escorted the judge's procession

Jerry-go-nimble-show: circus

Jockey to the Fair: popular eighteenth-century folk-song

John Knox: Calvinist priest (*c.* 1505–72), who is chiefly remembered for his uncompromising criticism of Mary, Queen of Scots

Jove: another name for Jupiter, the chief of the Roman gods

Juggernaut: idol of Vishnu, a Hindu god. Worshippers used to throw themselves under the wheels of the car that carried it

Jumping-jack: probably a jack-in-the-box

Juno: female head of the Roman gods

Keats: John Keats (1795–1821), the English romantic poet. A 'too happy happiness' is adapted from a line in his 'Ode to a Nightingale' (1820)

Knight-service: service due to a lord by his knights in the medieval period

Laban: father of Leah and Rachel (Genesis xxix: 16)

Lady Day: 25 March, the day when new contracts for employment or tenancies were issued

Lammas: 1 August

Lammocken: lounging or slouching

Lanceolate: shaped like the head of a spear

Laodicean neutrality: in Revelations iii: 14–22 the Laodicean church is reprimanded for its indifference

Lead . . . gloom: quotation from John Henry Newman's famous hymn (1833)

Let your light so shine: the words of the Offertory during Holy Communion (Matthew v: 16)

Lettre-de-cachet: official order for imprisonment or arrest, originally from French king. The command could not be refused

Leveller: death

Lied like a Cretan: in the ancient world, the Cretans were known as thieves and liars

Lief: ready, glad

Like a Samson: of great strength (see Judges xiii–xvi)

Like a thief in the night: see I Thessalonians v: 2

Like ghosts from an enchanter fleeing: quotation from Shelley's 'Ode to the West Wind' (1819)

Limber: frail

Logician's list: rational deductions

Long-headed: cunning, intelligent

Long-hundreds: six score

Louvre-boards: boards so arranged in a slope as to protect from rain but to let in air and light

Love in a Village: comic opera written by Isaac Bickerstaffe (1762)

Lucina: Roman goddess of childbirth

Magpie all alone: omen of ill-luck

Maid of the Mill, The: light opera by Isaac Bickerstaffe (1765)

Maiden's Blush: a rose

Maid's Tragedy, The: by the Jacobean playwrights Francis Beaumont and John Fletcher (performed 1619)

Malbrook: 'Malbrouk, s'en va-t-en guerre', an eighteenth-century French rhyme

Malthouse: building in which barley malt is germinated by spreading. It was often the centre for local gatherings because of the warmth

Marlborough: English general (1650–1722)

Melpomene: in Greek mythology she was the Muse of tragedy

Milton's Satan: in Milton's epic poem *Paradise Lost* Satan sees Paradise from the Tree of Life (Book I V)

Minerva: Roman goddess of wisdom, war and the arts, credited with inventing the flute

Mnasylus: shepherd in the Roman poet Virgil's sixth *Eclogue*

Moorish arch: arch shaped like a horseshoe

Morton: he announces the death of Hotspur in Shakespeare's *Henry IV, Part I*

Moses in Horeb: in Exodus xvii: 6 water comes from the smitten rock

Moses left the presence of Pharaoh: in Exodus x: 28–9 Moses seeks the release of the children of Israel

Mourning Bride, The: tragedy by William Congreve (performed 1697)

Name a hent: give a hint

Napoleon at St Helena: the great French Emperor lived in exile there after his defeat at Waterloo until his death in 1821

Near: mean

Neshness: weakness

News-bell: singing in the ears, which supposedly indicates bad news to come

Nicholas Poussin: painter (1593/4–1665), generally regarded as having founded the Classical French school

Night Thoughts: The Complaint, or Night Thoughts on Life, Death and Im- *mortality*, a much reprinted poem on religion and death by Edward Young (published 1742–5)

Nijni Novgorod: Soviet city famous for its annual fair. Its present name is Gorky after the writer Maxim Gorky

Ninth plague of Egypt: see Exodus x: 22

Noachian: of Noah's time, meaning very old indeed

Non lucendo: acting in a contrary way

Nymphean tissue: like a goddess

Offish: aloof, stand-offish

Olympus: mountain home of the gods in Greek mythology

Palimpsest: manuscript that has been twice written on, some of the original being evident beneath the later writing

Palter: haggle or talk insincerely

Paradise Lost: the epic poem of the fall of man by John Milton (published 1667)

Passados: sabre thrusts

Pattens: overshoes with wooden soles

Pelican in the wilderness: 'I am become like a pelican in the wilderness' (Psalm cii: 6)

Penetralia: innermost parts

Phaeton: four-wheeled open carriage drawn by two horses

Phantom of delight: quotation from the poem 'She was a Phantom of Delight' by William Wordsworth (1807)

Philistines: boorish, uncultivated people

Picotees: carnations

Pilasters: decorative columns built into a wall

Pilgrim's Progress: an allegory by John Bunyan (published 1678, 1684)

Pillars of Hercules: in classical times the name for the mountains at the entrance to the Mediterranean, with Gibraltar on one side and Abyla on the other

Pinchbeck repeater: cheap metal watch named after the maker of the metal

Pipkin: pot

Pleiads: the constellation in Taurus

Plimmed: rose and fell

Points: charge

Prisoners' base: game in which two groups, in competition, try to capture – and thus imprison – anyone who leaves 'base'

Provence: cabbage rose

Pucker: confusion, chaos

Purification Day: Candlemas Day, 2 February

Quarter-jack: man's figure which mechanically strikes the bell of a clock every quarter of an hour

R A: Royal Academician

Rathe-ripe: an early ripening apple

Reck'd not her own rede: ignored her own advice. It is a reference to Ophelia's appeal to Laertes in *Hamlet* (I, iii)

Reed-drawing: pulling rough thatching reeds through a frame to smoothe them out

Regrater: middleman in trade, retailer

Rembrandt effects: contrasts between light and shade in painting, associated with the Dutch painter Rembrandt van Ryn (1606–69)

Rick-stick: implement for combing the thatch of the rick

Robinson Crusoe: a romance by Daniel Defoe (published 1719)

Roman cement: cement made by mixing chalk, clay, lime, sand and water

Rooted: uprooted

Rowel: spiked wheel on a spur, used to urge horses

Rumen: first and largest stomach of the sheep

Russia duck: strong linen for outer garments

Ruysdael: Jacob van Ruysdael (1628–82), a Dutch landscape painter

Saint-Simonian: socialist ideals and practices, so-called after the Comte de Saint Simon (1760–1825), the founder of socialism in France

Scanning measure: with equal emphasis on each syllable of the word

Scram: unimportant

Scroff: kindling

Scurr of whetting: noise of sharpening

Seeds of Love: seventeenth-century song

Serpent: a wind instrument of the cornet family, made from a wooden tube

Settle: seat with a high back for two or more

Sexajessamine Sunday: Sexagesima, the second Sunday before Lent

Shade: spirit, soul of the dead

Shadrach, Meshach, Abednego: Daniel's companions, who were rescued from the furnace to which they were condemned for refusing to worship the golden image of Nebuchadnezzar

Shearlings and hogs: sheep shorn once and those waiting to be shorn

Shimei, the son of Gera: see II Samuel xvi: 5–14

Shrewsbury: the battle fought between the rebels and the king in 1403

Siddim: a valley of bitumen pits in the area that is now the Dead Sea

Silenus: a Satyr in Greek mythology, frequently depicted as drunk

Skit: skittish horse

Smack-and-coddle: kiss and cuddle

Snap of victuals: light meal, snack

Snapper: sudden change to bad weather

Sortes Sanctorum: oracles of the Holy Scriptures. A method of fortune-telling in which the Bible was opened at random, the words on the page supposedly forecasting what will happen

Spars: U-shaped pegs used for holding down thatch

Spear-bed: bed of reeds

Spectator, The: celebrated magazine edited by Richard Steele and Joseph Addison (1711–12)

Spreading-board: board on which the sheep are placed for shearing

Spring waggon: light cart mounted on springs

St John Long: John St John Long (1798–1834), Irish doctor, who died of tuberculosis after refusing to take his own quack remedies

St Vitus's dance: disease that causes lack of muscular control, seen in the jerking movements of those who suffer from it

Staddles: supports for corn or hay stacks

Stale in wedlock: married for some time

Stales: cakes that are not fresh

Stoic: having self-control, accepting adversity, from the ancient Greek school of philosophy

Stone saddles: supports on which a rick is built

Store ewes: sheep kept for fattening up

Stump bedstead: bed without posts

Stun-poll: blockhead

Summer's farewell: the Michaelmas daisy

Surrogate: the representative of the bishop

Swashing: dashing, swaggering

Swoln with wind . . . drew: quotation from John Milton's poem *Lycidas* (1637)

Syllogisms: kind of reasoning by which conclusions are derived from two propositions

Takings: temper, moods

Terburg: Gerard Terburg (1716–81), Dutch painter

Tergiversation: i.e. retracting her promise

Terrible Ten: the Ten Commandments

Τετέλεσται: 'It is finished'. Christ's last words on the Cross (John xxix: 30)

Thatching-beetle: wooden mallet for knocking in thatch

Thesmothete: law-giver, from the Greek

Thirtover: contrary

Thompson's Wonderfuls: type of potato

Thor: Norse god of thunder

Three-double: folded in three

Tined: shut

Tom King: highwayman and friend of Dick Turpin, who accidentally killed him

Tom Putt: variety of apple from the area

Tophet: place near Jerusalem associated with human sacrifices (see II Kings xxiii: 10)

Traitor's Gate: gate at the river entrance to the Tower of London

Traypse: to go

Tressy oat-ears: like braided hair

Trochar: lance-like tool in a tube for probing the stomach of flatulent sheep

Turner: J MW Turner (1775–1851), the celebrated landscape painter

Turnpike-gate: point on the road where users had to pay a toll towards the maintenance of the road

Tuscany: type of rose, deep crimson in colour

Tything: in Saxon times, a division of ten households, which held a communal responsibility

Uncertain glory of an April day: quotation from Shakespeare's *Two Gentlemen of Verona* (I, iii)

Union: workhouse built by the parishes to house the homeless and improvident

Use-money: interest gained from charitable bequests

Vandyked: collar with long points. The association is derived from the collars in portraits by the seventeenth-century painter Vandyke

Vanity of Human Wishes, The: poem by Samuel Johnson (published 1749)

Vashti: wife of King Ahasuerus. She was deposed to make way for Esther

Venus: Roman goddess of love

Vermiculations: decorations of wormlike curvings or marks

Vestal: one of the virgin priestesses who guarded the sacred fire in the Vesta temple in Rome

Walkingame's Arithmetic: first published in 1751, and used by Hardy early in his schooldays

Ware: beware

Warming-pans: Long-handled vessels filled with hot coals to warm the sheets of the bed

Whop and slap: work enthusiastically

Wimble: hand tool for boring holes

Wimbling haybonds: twisting the hay into ropes

Windrows: long rows of raked hay

Wish her cake dough: wish she could be as she was before

Woman whose heart ... nets: see Ecclesiastes vii: 26

Yeaning: lambing

Discussion Topics and Examination Questions

DISCUSSION TOPICS

Your understanding and appreciation of the novel will be much increased if you discuss aspects of it with other people. Here are some of the topics you can consider:

1. How far was Bathsheba responsible for her own suffering and the suffering of others?

2. Discuss what you think might happen in the married life of Bathsheba and Gabriel. Do you foresee any problems?

3. Work out the number of coincidences in the novel and discuss their effect on the plot.

4. Which events in *Far from the Madding Crowd* do you find improbable and why? Select three or four incidents from the novel on which to base your discussions.

5. What part do the rustic characters play in the novel? You might think of about four or five of them, indicating clearly their main characteristics.

6. Do you find the novel pessimistic? Think about any aspects of it that make you feel the author has a depressing view of life.

7. In what ways does nature play an important part in the novel? Consider three or four particular scenes.

8. How would you set about defending Sergeant Troy from the accusation that he is thoroughly selfish?

9. Discuss the part played by Liddy in the novel.

10. 'Boldwood is his own worst enemy.' How far do you agree or disagree with this judgement?

11. 'Too good to be true.' Is this a fair description of Gabriel?

12. 'The happy ending is unnatural.' How far do you agree or disagree with this statement?

THE GCSE EXAMINATION

If you are studying for the GCSE examination you may find that the set texts have been selected by your teacher from a very wide list of suggestions in the examination syllabus. The questions in the examination paper will therefore be applicable to many different books. Here are some possible questions which you could answer by making use of *Far from the Madding Crowd*:

1. Have you read a novel or story in which an outsider influences and then changes the lives of other characters? Describe how he or she does this.

2. Some books deal with a sudden or impetuous action, which changes the course of events or lives. Show how this happens in the text of your choice.

3. In the book you are studying, show how any two characters are changed by their experiences.

4. In your chosen book, show how important are the sense of place

and setting.

5. What part does the unexpected play in one of the books you are studying? Select at least two incidents on which to base your answer.

6. In the book you are reading, show how the author contrasts characters and why.

7. For which character in the book you are studying do you feel most sympathy and why?

8. Write an account of the most dramatic incident in a book you are reading.

9. Examine any relationship in the book you are reading and show how it develops. Do you find it close to life or not?

FURTHER EXAMINATION QUESTIONS

1. With close reference to either *two* or *three* episodes in the novel, show how Hardy makes us aware of Bathsheba's development to maturity.

(*Associated Examining Board, 1984*)

2. How does his relationship with Fanny deepen our understanding of Troy's character?

(*Associated Examining Board, 1984*)

3. In *Far from the Madding Crowd*, trouble often seems to follow when people are not at work. Examine carefully the contribution to the plot made by three instances where you feel this is true, and discuss what Hardy's attitude might be towards the relationship between work and leisure as it is shown in this novel.

(*Associated Examining Board, 1985*)

4. In the opening chapter of *Far from the Madding Crowd*, Gabriel Oak is described as 'a man whose moral colour was a kind of pepper-and-salt mixture', suggesting that he is neither particularly good nor bad. How well does this description apply to the character of Gabriel Oak as it is revealed over the course of the novel?

(Associated Examining Board, 1985)

FOR THE BEST IN PAPERBACKS, LOOK FOR THE

In every corner of the world, on every subject under the sun, Penguin represents quality and variety – the very best in publishing today.

For complete information about books available from Penguin – including Pelicans, Puffins, Peregrines and Penguin Classics – and how to order them, write to us at the appropriate address below. Please note that for copyright reasons the selection of books varies from country to country.

In the United Kingdom: For a complete list of books available from Penguin in the U.K., please write to *Dept E.P., Penguin Books Ltd, Harmondsworth, Middlesex, UB7 0DA*

In the United States: For a complete list of books available from Penguin in the U.S., please write to *Dept BA, Penguin, 299 Murray Hill Parkway, East Rutherford, New Jersey 07073*

In Canada: For a complete list of books available from Penguin in Canada, please write to *Penguin Books Canada Ltd, 2801 John Street, Markham, Ontario L3R 1B4*

In Australia: For a complete list of books available from Penguin in Australia, please write to the *Marketing Department, Penguin Books Australia Ltd, P.O. Box 257, Ringwood, Victoria 3134*

In New Zealand: For a complete list of books available from Penguin in New Zealand, please write to the *Marketing Department, Penguin Books (NZ) Ltd, Private Bag, Takapuna, Auckland 9*

In India: For a complete list of books available from Penguin, please write to *Penguin Overseas Ltd, 706 Eros Apartments, 56 Nehru Place, New Delhi, 110019*

In Holland: For a complete list of books available from Penguin in Holland, please write to *Penguin Books Nederland B.V., Postbus 195, NL–1380AD Weesp, Netherlands*

In Germany: For a complete list of books available from Penguin, please write to *Penguin Books Ltd, Friedrichstrasse 10 – 12, D–6000 Frankfurt Main 1, Federal Republic of Germany*

In Spain: For a complete list of books available from Penguin in Spain, please write to *Longman Penguin España, Calle San Nicolas 15, E–28013 Madrid, Spain*

FOR THE BEST IN PAPERBACKS, LOOK FOR THE

PENGUIN PASSNOTES

This comprehensive series, designed to help O-level, GCSE and CSE students, includes:

SUBJECTS
Biology
Chemistry
Economics
English Language
Geography
Human Biology
Mathematics
Modern Mathematics
Modern World History
Narrative Poems
Nursing
Physics

SHAKESPEARE
As You Like It
Henry IV, Part I
Henry V
Julius Caesar
Macbeth
The Merchant of Venice
A Midsummer Night's Dream
Romeo and Juliet
Twelfth Night

LITERATURE
Arms and the Man
Cider With Rosie
Great Expectations
Jane Eyre
Kes
Lord of the Flies
A Man for All Seasons
The Mayor of Casterbridge
My Family and Other Animals
Pride and Prejudice
The Prologue to The Canterbury
    Tales
Pygmalion
Saint Joan
She Stoops to Conquer
Silas Marner
To Kill a Mockingbird
War of the Worlds
The Woman in White
Wuthering Heights

FOR THE BEST IN PAPERBACKS, LOOK FOR THE 🐧

PENGUIN MASTERSTUDIES

This comprehensive list, designed for advanced level and first-year under-graduate studies, includes:

SUBJECTS
Applied Mathematics
Biology
Drama: Text into Performance
Geography
Pure Mathematics

LITERATURE
Absalom and Achitophel
Barchester Towers
Dr Faustus
Eugénie Grandet
The Great Gatsby
Gulliver's Travels
Joseph Andrews
The Mill on the Floss
A Passage to India
Persuasion *and* Emma
Portrait of a Lady
Tender Is the Night
Vanity Fair
The Waste Land

CHAUCER
The Knight's Tale
The Miller's Tale
The Nun's Priest's Tale
The Pardoner's Tale
The Prologue to The Canterbury
   Tales
A Chaucer Handbook

SHAKESPEARE
Antony & Cleopatra
Hamlet
King Lear
Measure for Measure
Much Ado About Nothing
Othello
The Tempest
A Shakespeare Handbook

'Standing somewhere between the literal, word-by-word explication of more usual notes and the abstractions of an academic monograph, the Masterstudies series is an admirable introduction to mainstream literary criticism for A Level students, in particular for those contemplating reading English at university. More than that, it is also a model of what student notes can achieve' – *The Times Literary Supplement*

FOR THE BEST IN PAPERBACKS, LOOK FOR THE 🐧

PENGUIN CLASSICS

Arnold Bennett	The Old Wives' Tale
Joseph Conrad	Heart of Darkness
	Nostromo
	The Secret Agent
	The Shadow-Line
	Under Western Eyes
E. M. Forster	Howard's End
	A Passage to India
	A Room With a View
	Where Angels Fear to Tread
Thomas Hardy	The Distracted Preacher and Other Tales
	Far From the Madding Crowd
	Jude the Obscure
	The Mayor of Casterbridge
	The Return of the Native
	Tess of the d'Urbervilles
	The Trumpet Major
	Under the Greenwood Tree
	The Woodlanders
Henry James	The Aspern Papers and The Turn of the Screw
	The Bostonians
	Daisy Miller
	The Europeans
	The Golden Bowl
	An International Episode and Other Stories
	Portrait of a Lady
	Roderick Hudson
	Washington Square
	What Maisie Knew
	The Wings of the Dove
D. H. Lawrence	The Complete Short Novels
	The Plumed Serpent
	The Rainbow
	Selected Short Stories
	Sons and Lovers
	The White Peacock
	Women in Love

FOR THE BEST IN PAPERBACKS, LOOK FOR THE ⊕

PENGUIN CLASSICS

Klaus von Clausewitz	On War
Friedrich Engels	The Origins of the Family, Private Property and the State
Wolfram von Eschenbach	Parzival
	Willehalm
Goethe	Elective Affinities
	Faust
	Italian Journey 1786–88
Jacob and Wilhelm Grimm	Selected Tales
E. T. A. Hoffmann	Tales of Hoffmann
Henrik Ibsen	The Doll's House/The League of Youth/The Lady from the Sea
	Ghosts/A Public Enemy/When We Dead Wake
	Hedda Gabler/The Pillars of the Community/The Wild Duck
	The Master Builder/Rosmersholm/Little Eyolf/John Gabriel Borkman/Peer Gynt
Søren Kierkegaard	Fear and Trembling
Friedrich Nietzsche	Beyond Good and Evil
	Ecce Homo
	A Nietzsche Reader
	Thus Spoke Zarathustra
	Twilight of the Idols and The Anti-Christ
Friedrich Schiller	The Robbers and Wallenstein
Arthur Schopenhauer	Essays and Aphorisms
Gottfried von Strassburg	Tristan
August Strindberg	Inferno and From an Occult Diary

Anton Chekhov	The Duel and Other Stories
	The Kiss and Other Stories
	Lady with Lapdog and Other Stories
	Plays (The Cherry Orchard/Ivanov/The Seagull/Uncle Vanya/The Bear/The Proposal/A Jubilee/Three Sisters
	The Party and Other Stories
Fyodor Dostoyevsky	The Brothers Karamazov
	Crime and Punishment
	The Devils
	The Gambler/Bobok/A Nasty Story
	The House of the Dead
	The Idiot
	Netochka Nezvanova
	Notes From Underground and The Double
Nikolai Gogol	Dead Souls
	Diary of a Madman and Other Stories
Maxim Gorky	My Apprenticeship
	My Childhood
	My Universities
Mikhail Lermontov	A Hero of Our Time
Alexander Pushkin	Eugene Onegin
	The Queen of Spades and Other Stories
Leo Tolstoy	Anna Karenin
	Childhood/Boyhood/Youth
	The Cossacks/The Death of Ivan Ilyich/Happy Ever After
	The Kreutzer Sonata and Other Stories
	Master and Man and Other Stories
	Resurrection
	The Sebastopol Sketches
	War and Peace
Ivan Turgenev	Fathers and Sons
	First Love
	Home of the Gentry
	A Month in the Country
	On the Eve
	Rudin
	Sketches from a Hunter's Album
	Spring Torrents